ADAM STEPAN

PCDEG

9179930505

YOUTUBE SECRETS

D1255066

YOUTUBE SECRETS

THE ULTIMATE GUIDE TO GROWING YOUR FOLLOWING AND MAKING MONEY AS A VIDEO INFLUENCER

SEAN CANNELL & BENJI TRAVIS

LIONCREST
PUBLISHING

YOUTUBE SECRETS

The Ultimate Guide to Growing Your Following and Making Money as a Video Influencer

SECOND EDITION

ISBN   978-1-5445-1181-8 *Paperback*
       978-1-5445-1182-5 *Ebook*

This book is dedicated to the Video Influencers and Think Media communities. Your stories of sacrifice, hustle, and persistence inspire and encourage us every day. Together we can impact the world through the power of online video, and we are grateful to be on the journey with you.

CONTENTS

SPREAD THE WORD AND WIN A FREE COACHING SESSION!

We'd love to feature your photos and posts about *YouTube Secrets*.

Just include the hashtag #YouTubeSecrets when posting photos and videos on your favorite social media network. When you share an image or video, you'll be entered to win a free personal coaching session with @BenjiManTV and @SeanCannell.

Thanks for the support!

PREFACE

—SEAN CANNELL & BENJI TRAVIS,
AUTHORS OF *YOUTUBE SECRETS*

YouTube remains the most dominant social media platform. That's not our opinion; that's a fact. According to new data from Pew Research, some 81 percent of Americans use YouTube compared to 69 percent who use Facebook, and YouTube continues to see significant growth around the world.[1]

When we wrote the first edition of *YouTube Secrets*, we had already experienced the life-changing power of YouTube in our own lives and observed it in the lives of others. We had a hunch that YouTube would continue to grow and

---

[1] Peter Suciu, "YouTube Remains the Most Dominant Social Media Platform," *Forbes*, April 7, 2021, https://www.forbes.com/sites/petersuciu/2021/04/07/youtube-remains-the-most-dominant-social-media-platform.

that more opportunities would unfold over the next few years. It seemed to us that YouTube still had plenty of open-door opportunities for everyday creators to build communities, impact people with their content, and make incredible income from home by starting and growing successful channels.

However, it turns out we weren't dreaming even close to big enough. New data that you'll read about in the introduction of this second edition reveals that the growth of YouTube has caught a fresh wave of momentum and is poised to reverberate around the world over the next decade. There are more opportunities than ever.

Of course, we're fully aware that new creators face serious challenges. Indeed, you might be wondering, *Is it too late to start a channel? Isn't there too much competition?* Maybe you started posting videos, but you've become frustrated that you're not getting views, or you've hit a growth plateau. Maybe you're overwhelmed trying to figure out camera tech and video editing. You may lack confidence, and you keep telling yourself, *I'm not smart enough, experienced enough, or talented enough to succeed on YouTube.*

If you feel discouraged, burnt out, or overwhelmed, we don't blame you. Besides the normal challenges of growing a channel on YouTube, we've just come through a global pandemic, and we're now facing an economic recession, ongoing health care challenges, extreme political divisions, inflation, and massive changes in the job market.

While you may have been knocked down, you don't have to stay down because buried in every crisis is a hidden opportunity. More than half of the people on Earth now use social media.[2] The global pandemic shifted our culture and habits, causing social media and online video consumption to skyrocket, triggering a digital and online shopping explosion.[3] As one expert revealed, "In years to come, we will look back at 2020 as the moment that changed everything. Nowhere else has unprecedented and unforeseen growth occurred as in the digital and e-commerce sectors, which have boomed amid the COVID-19 crisis."[4]

We all know this from experience. Some people who had never shopped online were forced to embrace it during the pandemic. Suddenly, even our parents and grandparents were ordering groceries, clothes, medicine, and other items through websites and apps. This has led to

2   "More than Half of the People on Earth Now Use Social Media," Hootsuite, July 21, 2020, https://www.hootsuite.com/newsroom/press-releases/more-than-half-of-the-people-on-earth-now-use-social-media.

3   Suzin Wold, "COVID-19 is Changing How, Why, and How Much We're Using Social Media," September 16, 2020, https://www.digitalcommerce360.com/2020/09/16/covid-19-is-changing-how-why-and-how-much-were-using-social-media/.

4   "How COVID-19 Triggered the Digital and E-commerce Turning Point," UNCTAD, March 15, 2021, https://unctad.org/news/how-covid-19-triggered-digital-and-e-commerce-turning-point.

remarkable growth in e-commerce, and there's a lot more room for growth in the years ahead as online shopping becomes even more widespread.

The rapidly growing e-commerce industry is already worth $4 trillion, so the financial opportunity is enormous. As we will discuss in depth in Chapter 6, as online shopping increases, YouTube creators have more opportunities to make money. It's called *affiliate marketing*, and it's one of the major ways creators are achieving financial success on YouTube. That means you get a cut of that $4 trillion pie, and since it's all online, you can tap into it from anywhere in the world.

Many people already have. Since we wrote the first edition of this book, millions have started YouTube channels and created a part-time and full-time living. In fact, a recent study revealed that being a content creator is now the fastest growing small business type.[5]

We've received countless emails and direct messages from readers of *YouTube Secrets* who have used our principles and strategies to overcome fear and start channels of their own. Business owners, leaders, and professional service providers are using the "Seven Cs" framework from *YouTube Secrets* to grow their revenue and scale

5   Yuanling Yuan and Josh Constine, "SignalFire's Creator Economy Market Map," SignalFire, July 8, 2021, https://signalfire.com/blog/creator-economy/.

their businesses, and many of them have crossed the 100,000-subscriber mark and received the coveted Silver Play button from YouTube for hitting that milestone. Many are also earning from $1,000 to over $10,000 a month from YouTube revenue alone. You'll hear their stories in this updated version of the book.

As you know, we are living in times of rapid change, and YouTube has continued to evolve over the past few years. While the foundational principles of success remain the same, the platform and the overall landscape of the creator economy have shifted. That's why we decided to put together this massively expanded second edition of *YouTube Secrets*.

We've completely overhauled the book with new data, new case studies, and new chapters that will give you an edge when it comes to what's working right now on YouTube. We've tweaked some of the tips and completely removed a few outdated strategies so you can feel confident that you're holding a reliable roadmap for achieving your YouTube goals.

We are in a new decade full of new opportunities on YouTube, but like William Arthur Ward said, "Opportunities are like sunrises. If you wait too long, you miss them."

So, turn the page and we'll guide you step-by-step on your journey to YouTube success.

INTRODUCTION

When most people think of YouTube, they still think of cat videos, viral memes, and homemade videos. In reality, there is a secret community of people on YouTube who are turning their creativity into careers, amassing huge followings, and creating lives on their own terms.

CNBC shared the story of Karina Garcia, known as the internet's Slime Queen. In less than three years, the twenty-three-year-old turned her one-time hobby posting do-it-yourself (DIY) slime videos into a full-time career and went from waitressing to making millions. While her story might have seemed crazy a decade ago, it's becoming more and more common.[6]

---

6   Courtney Connley, "This 23-Year-Old Went from Waitressing to Earning Millions as YouTube's 'Slime Queen,'" CNBC, January 31, 2018, https://www.cnbc.com/2018/01/30/this-former-waitress-is-earning-millions-as-youtubes-slime-queen.html.

Imagine if you'd told your family and friends a decade ago that you wanted to make a living as a YouTube creator. Chances are, you would have been asked, "Why don't you get a real job?" Today, there is no debate. Being a YouTube creator *is* a real job. After all, YouTube generated $19.7 billion in revenue in 2020, and roughly half of that revenue goes directly into the pockets of everyday people like you who upload their videos to the platform.[7]

According to an article in *SignalFire,* being a YouTube creator has "become the fastest-growing type of small business." Tens of thousands of channels are earning seven-figure incomes, but new data reveals that over a million are earning six figures. Millions more earn five figures. All of these numbers are expected to double in the next few years.[8]

By the way, ad revenue is only one of the ways YouTube creators are monetizing their content. Later in this book, we'll share many other ways you can make money through online videos. It's a revolution. You may be hearing about it for the first time, but this is a very real opportunity. Regular, everyday people from all walks of life are discovering the power of building influence, creating income, and

---

7   Mansoor Iqbal, "YouTube Revenue and Usage Statistics (2022)," Business of Apps, January 11, 2022, https://www.businessofapps.com/data/youtube-statistics/#6.

8   Yuanand Constine, "SignalFire's Creator Economy Market Map."

making a massive impact on YouTube by creating content based on their hobbies, passions, and professional lives.

Laura Vitale's passion is cooking, and she always dreamed of writing a cookbook. She started her YouTube channel shortly after quitting a restaurant job, making videos with her husband in her own kitchen. Ten years later, she had grown her channel to such an extent that she landed a position on Food Network as a regular host and got a book deal for her cookbook. She's now a bestselling author, due in large part to amassing 3.8 million subscribers on her channel, and she has become one of the most highly recognized food personalities on the platform.

John Kohler, a passionate gardener, has one of the most highly watched gardening shows on YouTube, *Growing Your Greens*. The first video he uploaded in 2009 was shot in one take, wasn't high definition, had no editing, and he wasn't even in the shot, but he had an obvious passion for gardening. Fifteen hundred videos later, with over one hundred million views and eight hundred thousand subscribers, he's a little savvier about video, but more importantly, he is using his channel to grow his core business: selling juicing machines.

Then there's Glen Henry, a.k.a. "Beleaf in Fatherhood," a father of four children who started posting vlogs documenting his parenting journey. After a few years of hard work, his commitment to consistency on YouTube and continuous learning paid off. He had the opportunity to work with Dove Men+Care, and he was in a feature film, *Dads,* on Apple TV+ alongside celebrities like Will Smith and Neil Patrick Harris.[9]

Through YouTube, he has built a powerful business and brand and hired a team to help him in his mission to equip fathers, give hope to mothers, and inspire children. And it all started by punching fear in the face and pressing record on his smartphone.

We're not saying everyone is going to become wealthy on YouTube. For some people, that might not even be their ambition. What's exciting is how people are taking their passions and hobbies and using them to create communities, connect with like-minded people, and make some money for themselves and their families.

Heather Torres is a great example of this. A homeschool mom with three kids, she started a homeschooling channel to share tips with other parents. After a year of posting videos in her spare time, her channel grew to over eighteen thousand subscribers, and her videos have been viewed over a million times. As a result, she has created

---

9   Diane J. Cho, "Beleaf in Fatherhood's Glen Henry on the Power of Parenthood: 'My Children Helped Me Become a Man,'" *People*, February 17, 2021, https://people.com/parents/how-i-parent-beleaf-in-fatherhood-glen-henry/.

a side income for her family and opened many doors of opportunity.

Now, you might be thinking, "These people started early. It's too late now. YouTube is crowded and there's too much competition." That's simply not the case. There are countless examples of creators of all ages, backgrounds, and ethnicities—from countries around the world—who have built successful and profitable YouTube channels.

YouTube was the number one most visited site on the internet in 2020! There's a massive audience looking for new creators and fresh content. That means now is a great time to get started. Don't put it off any longer.[10]

Additionally, you might assume that all of these successful YouTubers had startup funding. Maybe you lack the money to buy the kind of expensive equipment people use to make professional TV shows. The good news is you don't need any of that. All the equipment you need to make compelling YouTube content is in your pocket right now, contained in your smartphone, a device that can create and upload high-definition (HD), even 4K, video.

Some people fear they don't have the talent to create quality YouTube content, but talent is not the number one require-

---

[10] "The Most Visited Internet Sites of 2020," Broadband Search, July 8, 2021, https://www. broadbandsearch.net/blog/most-visited-popular-websites.

ment on YouTube. Things like passion, excitement, fun, information, education, and answering people's questions are far more important. The most successful creators today aren't talented in the ways that Hollywood stars are. In fact, many of them are introverts in regular life, but they have a passion for the content they create. That's the real secret of YouTube. If you're passionate enough to help others and excited enough to keep their interest, you're ready.

Successful influencers on YouTube are just average, everyday folks who care about something and have developed some skill or knowledge about a subject, whether it's fitness, faith, or decluttering a home. Any kind of interest or hobby can become valuable content without the need for fancy editing or an ultratalented creator.

WHY VIDEO?

In general, we all prefer to connect and do business with people we know, like, and trust. The problem with connecting online is that it's harder to look someone in the eye, have a real conversation with them, and gauge their facial expressions. This is particularly true with blogging but also holds true for audio content. That's one reason we believe video is absolutely the best way to communicate any message.

Through video, it's much easier for an audience to get

to know and trust you. The most successful YouTubers have regular viewers who feel like they have developed a friendship with them. Only video engages people on that level.

They say a picture is worth a thousand words, but digital marketing expert James McQuivey of Forrester Research estimates that a single minute of video content is equivalent to 1.8 million words.[11] For anyone who has a message, dream, business, brand, or something they want to get out to the world, video is the most effective way to do it.

Video is also growing like crazy. Almost every social media platform has adopted video as its preferred medium. Can you think of a single social media platform that hasn't already incorporated video? And, indeed, more video content is being watched now than ever before. Statistics reveal that 85 percent of all internet users in the United States watch online video content monthly on their devices. That's a 30 percent increase since the publication of the first edition of this book![12]

Is competition increasing on YouTube? For sure. But so is demand! Recent data reveals that the demand for

---

11   James McQuivey, "How Video Will Take Over the World," Forrester, June 17, 2008, https://www.forrester.com/report/How-video-Will-Take-Over-The-World/RES44199.

12   Maryam Mohsin, "10 Video Marketing Statistics That You Need to Know in 2020," Oberlo, March 30, 2020, https://www.datatech.guru/archives/1587.

video content is growing at a rapid rate. The time people spend watching videos online is increasing, and all signs currently suggest that this trend will continue. Already, audiences under the age of thirty-six spend more time watching videos online than on traditional broadcast mediums such as television. It's estimated that by 2022, 82 percent of global internet traffic will come from video streaming and downloads.[13]

WHY YOUTUBE?

Why is YouTube the best video platform for creating impact? According to the latest statistics, the video-sharing platform has 2.3 billion users worldwide.[14] That's four times the population of North America.

YouTube is also the second-most-popular search engine after Google. It receives more searches per month than Microsoft Bing, Yahoo, AOL, and Ask.com combined. YouTube viewers watch over one billion hours of videos on the platform every single day and are responsible for generating billions and billions of views. Do the math. If every single person on Earth watched videos, that would translate to roughly 8.4 minutes per person per day.

13 Ben Munson, "Video Will Account for 82% of All Internet Traffic by 2022, Cisco Says," Fierce Video, November 27, 2018,https://www.fiercevideo.com/video/video-will-account-for-82-all-internet-traffic-by-2022-cisco-says.

14 Maryam Mohsin, "10 YouTube Stats Every Marketer Should Know in 2021 [Infographic]," Oberlo, January 25, 2021, https://www.oberlo.com/blog/youtube-statistics.

Also, Google owns YouTube, so search functionality lies at its heart. That makes YouTube distinct from other social media platforms. Facebook, Twitter, Instagram, and TikTok aren't search engines, so YouTube provides a distinct advantage in getting discovered and building your influence online.

YouTube is not only available but also localized in over a hundred countries, which means the platform adapts to different languages in each of the markets it is in. Plus, it can be accessed in eighty different languages, ranging from the world's most spoken languages like English, Spanish, and Mandarin to more obscure ones like Azerbaijani, Khmer, and Laotian.

Whatever your business, brand, interest, or hobby, a target audience is looking for your content on YouTube. Maybe it's someone seeking advice on growing healthier tomatoes, applying smoky eye shadow, tips on cryptocurrency, or saving money on taxes. YouTube gives you immediate access to a worldwide audience.

YouTube is also free. Plenty of tools will help you create content, but YouTube has no financial barrier. You can upload unlimited HD and even 4K content to your channel at no cost. Think about how much harder it was to get a message out to a worldwide audience twenty years ago. Back then, you probably would have had to buy television airtime, which would have cost a fortune. YouTube has completely leveled the playing field. An average person with a smartphone can reach the whole world on a platform packed with features. Don't take how amazing this is for granted. You have access to one of the greatest opportunities for outreach in *history*.

YouTube also pays well. In our experience, if you want to monetize your video content, YouTube provides the most lucrative opportunity. The most obvious means of making money is through ad revenue, which Google shares with content creators, but that's not the only way to profit. Brands routinely pay to have their products featured on YouTube because they trust the platform. Brand sponsorship, in fact, is one of your channel's biggest monetary opportunities.

New data also reveals that the YouTube economy is incredibly healthy and strong, despite the challenges of the global coronavirus pandemic. The number of new channels that joined the YouTube Partner Program (YPP) in 2020 more than doubled over the previous year!

As Susan Wojcicki revealed in an "Inside YouTube" article:

> Creators are building next generation media companies that impact the economy's overall success. According to an Oxford Economics report, YouTube's

creative ecosystem contributed approximately $16 billion to the US GDP in 2019, supporting the equivalent of 345,000 full time jobs. We're also seeing real impact in other countries around the globe. The UK in 2019 saw approximately £1.4 billion contributed to the British GDP and the equivalent of 30,000 full time jobs. And in France, there was an estimated €515 million contributed to the French GDP and the equivalent of 15,000 full time jobs.[15]

No other social media network offers such easy revenue-sharing, certainly not with YouTube's quality or infrastructure. Every day, more and more people are building influential and lucrative channels. In 2010, YouTube's fifth birthday, there were only five channels that had one million subscribers.[16] Fast-forward to today, and there are over twenty-three thousand.[17] The number continues to grow rapidly. According to a recent stat from Think with Google, there are 75 percent more channels with over a million subscribers this year compared to last

---

15 Susan Wojcicki, "Letter from Susan: Our 2021 Priorities," YouTube, January 26, 2021, https://blog.youtube/inside-youtube/letter-from-susan-our-2021-priorities.

16 Sam Gutelle, "There Are Now 2,000 YouTube Channels With At Least One Million Subscribers, *Tubefilter,* April 4, 2016, https://www.tubefilter.com/2016/04/04/youtube-millionaires-2000-channels/.

17 Jacob Bates, "How Many YouTube Channels Have Over 1 Million Subscribers," Data Driven Investor, January 7, 2021, https://medium.datadriveninvestor.com/how-many-youtube-channels-have-over-1-million-subscribers-56881000f35a.

year.[18] It might astound you to learn that so many people have turned their channels into real jobs and full-time careers, but it's happening right now.

OUR BEGINNINGS

By now, you might be asking yourself, "Who are Sean and Benji, and what makes them experts on YouTube? Why should I listen to them?" When we first met over a decade ago, we both already had a few years' experience on YouTube, but we were also at the lowest points of our financial lives. In the years that followed, as a result of the opportunities provided by YouTube, we were able to create full-time incomes and build thriving seven-figure businesses off our individual efforts. Benji has been able to raise $2 million for charity through live broadcast video and built an income off Google AdSense and brand sponsorships through vlogging.

Benji, who started out behind the scenes with no video production experience, has been vlogging with his wife Judy for over a decade, gaining over 1.8 million subscribers and a billion video views. He has been able to turn their passions into a seven-figure business.

---

18 "YouTube User Stats from Brandcast 2017: 3 Trends in Video Viewing Behavior," Think with Google, May 2017, https://www.thinkwithgoogle.com/marketing-strategies/video/youtube-user-stats-video-viewing-behavior-trends/.

As for Sean, he is a small-town kid and college dropout who started shooting videos in his bedroom (by the way, they were terrible). Today, his YouTube channel, *Think Media*, has grown to over 1.8 million subscribers and become one of the fastest-growing YouTube startup companies, generating over eight figures in revenue.

One day six years ago, as we were discussing some of the insights and lessons we had learned from building our individual channels, we came up with the idea to share this information with the rest of the world. This book is a result of that decision. Of course, we wanted to test and prove that our frameworks and theories worked before we started teaching them to others. That led to the creation of our *Video Influencers* channel. We managed to grow *Video Influencers* to over ten million views and 250,000 subscribers before publishing the first edition of the book. But the growth hasn't stopped. Today *Video Influencers* has over 660,000 subscribers and more than 575 videos that have generated more than thirty-two million video views.

Our stories bear many similarities to the success stories of other YouTubers. We were regular people with a passion for something, and by consistently delivering value on that subject, we built an audience. Our success didn't come from being super-talented. It came from sharing basic principles that anybody can follow to build influence, income, and impact with online video.

In this book, we will reveal the paths, principles, tips, steps, and strategies that anybody can use to reach an audience, make money, build a business or personal brand, and share their message with the world. The lessons we've learned come from our twenty years of combined experience on the platform, as well as more than a hundred interviews we've conducted with successful YouTubers from all walks of life.

WHAT TO EXPECT

So where are we headed? In the first section of this book, we want to share with you the seven-step strategy that has worked for us since 2008. All the advice we give will be practical, with nothing beyond the average person's comprehension or skill level. Though the platform changes over time, our basic seven-step framework for YouTube success remains timeless.

One of the biggest mistakes people make when trying to build their influence online comes from focusing on short-term tactics that aren't part of an overall cohesive strategy, so in the second section, we'll cover specific tactics and secret hacks that are working right now to grow influence on YouTube. *Everything* has been updated for a new decade on YouTube, so you can be sure you're getting the best information. Plus, we've added two new chapters to help you win.

Finally, in the appendix, we will share some of the best resources out there, including videos, books, websites, tools, and apps. We'll also answer some of the most frequently asked questions about YouTube and online video. Topics covered will include when and how to scale your business, grow your team, pick the right camera, and deal with haters and trolls, and advice for becoming a daily vlogger.

Here's our suggestion for getting the most out of this book: read it through one time just to wrap your head around the cohesive strategy we lay out. Then, come back to it as a reference while growing your YouTube channel, digging in deeper on specific points. We have included links to videos for further training, so you can take your education to the next level.

We believe that anyone can create a part-time or even full-time income with YouTube, expand their reach, build a community, and get product or brand awareness through the strategies we provide. Maybe you just want more exposure for a cause, charity, or nonprofit, or maybe you're trying to create a community around a hobby. Is your dream to become financially free? Maybe you dream of becoming a superstar. Whatever the case, we'll give you the techniques you need to make it happen. In concrete terms, this means more subscribers, more followers, and more income.

We can't promise that you'll become a famous YouTuber, but we can share every principle we've utilized to create our own success, as well as the secrets we've learned from some of today's top YouTube creators. By the end of this book, you will have a comprehensive yet simple guide for creating success for yourself, if you're willing to put in the effort.

So, turn the page, and let's get into the core strategy that's going to help you achieve success on YouTube.

PART ONE

• • •

STRATEGY: THE SEVEN Cs

In this section, we're going to share the essential building blocks for creating a successful YouTube channel. We call them The Seven Cs: *Courage, Clarity, Channel, Content, Community, Cash, and Consistency.* You'll learn everything from finding the inspiration for the idea behind your channel to the nuts and bolts of creating and releasing your content.

In each chapter, we'll feature real YouTubers and share stories from *Video Influencers* interviews. Through these examples, you'll see what the building blocks look like when put into practice, so that you can also begin to put them in place to create your own success story.

CHAPTER 1

• • •

COURAGE: IGNITE PASSION AND TRANSCEND FEAR

"You don't have to be great to start, but you have to start to be great."

—ZIG ZIGLAR

What keeps people from getting started on YouTube? Chiefly fear—that deer-in-the-headlights feeling. What are they afraid of? Being judged, getting hate comments and negativity, and putting effort into something and not getting any return.

The quickest way to get beyond the fear is to simply get started. Just go for it. Some of the fears are valid. You probably will get negativity and trolling, so prepare yourself mentally for that reality. Ultimately, you just have to go through with it, because not starting at all is worse than failure.

Once upon a time, Benji agreed to go skydiving if he raised a certain amount of money for his annual Dancember charity event. He'd never been skydiving before, so he was taking a risk. Lo and behold, the money was raised, so we both set off for Snohomish, Washington, and climbed into a small prop plane together.

We were shocked at how fast the little plane climbed. Once we achieved altitude, the instructor opened the door, and bodies just started dropping out of the plane one after the other. Needless to say, we were terrified. What if something went wrong? What if our chutes didn't open?

As we stood there in the plane, petrified, the instructor reminded us that, at the end of the day, there's no jumping out of a plane halfway. It's all or nothing. Benji went first. Seeing him jump didn't build Sean's confidence. If anything, he got even more scared watching Benji fall away from the plane, but the only way to deal with the fear was to join him.

Jumping out of a plane is intense. You flip around and spin, but eventually the parachute opens. Once that happens, the fear goes away. Ultimately, we realized everything was going to be okay, and we were thankful we'd gone through with it.

The YouTube experience feels similar. The only way to overcome all those initial fears and anxieties is to go through with it. It's the old Nike slogan: Just Do It. Or, as the old saying goes: "Courage is not the absence of fear; it's the willingness to act despite the fear."

You might sound awkward on camera initially. Some people will post negative comments. You will have a lot to learn. All these things are true, so make up your mind to push through them. At one point, every single person on YouTube was brand new, had never done it before, and had no subscribers. Every person on social media started at zero, but they summoned their courage and started posting and uploading content. That's what we did in the beginning. And that's what you have to do.

FIND YOUR "WHY"

Tapping into your "why" can help you overcome your fears. Simon Sinek writes in his well-known book, *Start with Why: How Great Leaders Inspire Everyone to Take Action*, "People don't buy what you do, they buy why you do it." Create a strong reason for being on YouTube.

Who do you want to inspire, encourage, educate, or help with your products and services? Who are the people you want to entertain? Figure that out and keep those people front and center. This will help you get over yourself. Motive is the root word of motivation: find a motive that is bigger than all the challenges it'll take to create your channel.

CULTIVATE MENTAL PREPARATION

Cultivating mental preparation is critical. If you're afraid you might get hate comments, prepare yourself for them. Accept that it's going to happen. Negative comments happen to every single YouTube creator. The only way to stop them is to turn off comments altogether, but that hinders engagement. In a way, negative comments are part of the beauty of YouTube. People can agree with you, and people can disagree with you. The more polarizing your content, the more strongly people will voice their opinions. Accept that fact going in.

The fear never goes away completely, but it does diminish over time, especially as you get better. When Benji created his first video, a steak-cooking tutorial, he definitely had that "deer-in-the-headlights" look. Anxiety about what viewers would think prevented him from acting like his natural, personable self. Over time, as he realized there were people who enjoyed his content, valued his videos, and wanted more, he got more comfortable in front of the camera. Facing the fear has resulted in over twenty-six million views on his food channel alone.

If you need a little encouragement getting started, go and check out that first video and see how far Benji has come: TubeSecretsBook.com/FirstVideos.

Sean started making videos for his church in 2003. At first, he was making a video every Wednesday for the youth group meeting, and then, after a year, he started making them for Sunday services as well. That was two videos a week, 104 videos a year, long before he got started on YouTube. As of today, he's created and posted well over three thousand videos.

His confidence comes from the sheer repetition of creating content. Despite this, he still has days where he's anxious about how people will respond to a video. On those days, remembering his "why" helps him punch fear in the face and keep pressing forward.

Fear continues to affect even the most seasoned YouTubers. Benji has a good friend who owns a very successful business. He started uploading videos on YouTube to promote the business, and over time, they helped grow it into a multimillion-dollar success story. However, after a while, he stopped uploading videos. When Benji asked him why, he said the negativity and hate comments he received killed his passion and creativity, despite his business's continued growth.

We aren't sharing this story to demotivate you. We just want to reiterate the fact that seasoned content creators all deal with this. Benji's friend wasn't mentally prepared for it, so it eventually became more than he could handle.

Another good friend of ours, Kandee Johnson, has been on YouTube since 2009, and now has millions of followers. She likes to say that, when it comes to hate comments, there's not a lot of truth in them. In fact, when she responds to hate comments, she often gets an apology or a confession in return. Many of the "trolls" tell her they never expected her to read their comment, and often they admit that the hate stems from something they're going through in their own lives. Rarely does it contain any real substance or negative judgment of her.

It's no surprise to us that this is a huge challenge for new creators. That's why we titled the first chapter, "Courage." If you're passionate about something, love to help people, and know this is what you want to do, have the courage to look beyond the negativity and trolls to see the vast community of people who need and want your content.

A COMMUNITY OF COURAGE

As you're summoning the courage to start your You-Tube channel, it's important to surround yourself with a community of courage. Friends and family might not understand your vision for wanting to build influence on YouTube. In mild cases, they'll feel indifference or confusion about your passion. In more severe cases, they might actively mock you. Develop patience. Beyond that, surround yourself with individuals who support you and can sustain and motivate you through the ups and downs.

One reason we wrote this book and created our channel was so we could put together a supportive community of like-minded Video Influencers who understand YouTube culture. We encourage you to attend meetups and conferences, to connect with relevant communities and fellow video creators in Facebook groups or online forums. These are the people who will strengthen you when you're dealing with challenges.

EXERCISE: YOUR MOTIVATION

As an exercise, think deeply about the following questions: What is your motivation for getting on YouTube? What do you hope to achieve through online video? What is your vision for your channel? Maybe you're hoping to create a side income for your family. Maybe you want to reach out to people with a particular message. Or maybe you're trying to create a community of like-minded people centered on a specific hobby or issue.

Once you have your answers to those questions, we recommend writing those answers down and posting them somewhere you'll often see them so you can stay focused throughout your YouTube journey. Be crystal clear in your answers. Any time fear, doubt, or discouragement creeps up on you, look at those answers and remind yourself of what is most important. Go back to the answers so that you can push through and continue building your channel.

After all, what is the opportunity cost of not taking action right now? If you were to ask any YouTube creator if they wish they had started ten years earlier, almost all of them would say yes. Even if they've achieved success, they would tell you they wish they'd started sooner.

What will your ten-years-from-now self think if you don't start now? Honestly, the best time to get started on YouTube was 2005, but the second-best time to get started is right now. What are you waiting for?

19   Mohsin, "10 YouTube Statistics Every Marketer Should Know in 2021 [Infographic]."

42 · YOUTUBE SECRETS

Myth #1: YouTube is too crowded.

Fact: According to the latest YouTube statistics, the video-sharing platform has 2.3 billion users worldwide as of 2021 and the growth is speeding up. There's room for you![19]

Myth #2: I don't have enough money.

Fact: These days, you can shoot, edit, and upload YouTube videos with the average smartphone, as long as you have an internet connection. Forget the fancy equipment and expensive gear.

Myth #3: I must be super-talented.

Fact: What matters most on YouTube is creating value for an audience with authenticity. If you can do that, you can find success. Start now and develop your skills as you go.

Myth #4: I don't have enough time.

Fact: In only a few hours a week, you can build a successful YouTube channel with consistent content.

Myth #5: I don't have enough connections.

Fact: It's not about connections. It's about content. All you have to do is create meaningful content and make it available.

Myth #6: Somebody already took my idea.

Fact: If someone is already doing what you want to do, that proves there's a market for it. McDonald's is not the only fast-food hamburger restaurant. There are hundreds of them. Why? Because people love burgers. You can find success with a subject even if others are already covering it.

CHAPTER 2

. . .

CLARITY: START WITH THE END IN MIND

"Start with the end outcome and work backwards to make your dream possible."

—WAYNE DYER

When you go to the airport to pick up a plane ticket, you have a destination in mind. You don't walk up to the ticket counter and say, "I'll just take a ticket to anywhere." Unfortunately, this is how many people treat their YouTube channel. If you don't know where you're going, if you have no end in mind, you'll wind up somewhere you may not even want to be.

At some point on your journey, preferably at the very beginning, you must ask yourself, "What is my goal for being on YouTube?" Are you trying to drive sales to your business? Would you like to build an audience? Is your goal to become famous? Do you want to build a community around your favorite hobby? Do you simply want to use it as a creative outlet?

Define what you want to get out of YouTube and make that the foundation of your channel.

THE THREE Ps

Something we hear a lot is, "I'm not really sure what my channel should be about or what my purpose on YouTube should be." If you're struggling to find an identity or purpose for your YouTube channel, we recommend building it at the intersection of passion, proficiency, and profit.

In Michael Hyatt's book, *Living Forward*, he speaks on passion. "To discover what you're passionate about," he writes, "ask yourself what you would do for free." What is something that lights you up, that isn't a short-term interest but something you firmly believe in and care about? What do you love? What will keep your interest? What fascinates you? What do you study? What do you read? Is it a real passion or just a current curiosity?

Think hard about this, because YouTube is a marathon, not a sprint. It's hard work. If you don't have deep love and passion for your channel, you will struggle to sustain your motivation through the ups and downs of building your influence on YouTube.

But passion alone is not enough. You also need proficiency. What have you developed a real skill in? What ability do other people respect or acknowledge in you?

When Sean was young, he served as an intern at his church for many years, and for a while, he wanted to be in music ministry. He loved to sing, and he wanted to play guitar. He even started getting lessons. However, he soon discovered that it wasn't his gift. He was passionate about it, but he wasn't proficient at it.

On the other hand, John Kohler, a gardening YouTuber with over 800,000 followers, is not only passionate about gardening—composting, organizing beds, juicing, and eating salads—but he has also developed his expertise on the subject over time. He has studied and learned all about it. Gardening is his life's work. He combines that passion and proficiency with a means to profit on YouTube, and he's thriving. John's YouTube channel is not about making money directly. Instead, he creates YouTube content to boost the buying audience for his juicing company.

The third P after passion and proficiency is profit. If you have passion and proficiency, but there isn't a market for it, all you have is a hobby, and if that's all you want then it's just fine. However, if you're trying to build a full-time income on YouTube, there must be a market for your chosen subject. You should probably do some market research to make sure you can build an audience. Otherwise, you may be dead in the water.

To build a sustainable business, you need all three: passion, proficiency, and profit. If you lack any of these, you might find success is just out of reach. If you have knowledge about your subject, if there's a market for it, but you have no passion for the subject, you could wind up hating your own success. If there is a market for it, and it's something you're passionate about, but you haven't developed proficiency yet, you probably won't have success. That doesn't mean you have to be the most knowledgeable person in the world. You don't have to be a world-renowned expert or have a degree in the subject matter. Just share what you know—what you want other people to know—from your own authentic perspective, and grow from there.

When you combine passion, proficiency, and profit, you find your niche, and you're one step closer to defining your end goal.

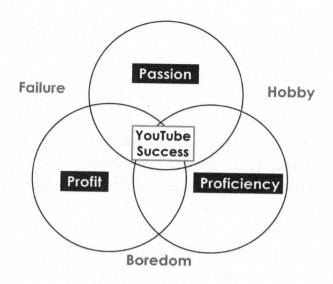

FINDING YOUR ZONE

When we started *Video Influencers*, our number one goal was to help people discover the life-changing power of online video and YouTube. We asked ourselves, "How can we reach the most people possible?" Initially, we thought the best way to deliver this information was through a book, but then our vision expanded. So, we put the book on hold and started the *Video Influencers* YouTube channel and social media accounts, and we started publishing content.

We recognized that, to impact people with our message, we needed to generate attention, awareness, and interest in this topic, so we set a goal of acquiring 100,000 subscribers on YouTube and 25,000 signed up for our email newsletter before we released the actual book. That way, when we launched this book, we would already have a community that had been impacted.

The channel grew beyond our wildest expectations. In fact, *Video Influencers* currently has over 650,000 subscribers on YouTube and over 100,000 people signed up for our email newsletter. We are excited to see so many people discovering the massive opportunity in the online video space and taking action to build their influence and income.

We set our end goal at day zero and used reverse engineering to create the necessary steps to reach it. We used the three Ps—passion, proficiency, and profit—did the hard work, built our audience, and the results followed.

Finding your zone means knowing the destination you want to reach so you can create your own roadmap to get there.

CLARIFYING YOUR CONTENT

Erik Conover wanted to travel the world full time, but he couldn't afford it. He decided to get the money to travel by making YouTube videos. He already had filmmaking experience, so he used that skill to set his end goal in motion. He started with vlogs set around popular destinations in New York City (where he lived at the time), directing his videos at tourists. Then, he leveraged his new audience to go on trips, at first paying for the trips himself, but eventually traveling all the time with his YouTube revenue. Within two years, Erik grew his audience from zero to three hundred thousand, and he now lives at the convergence of his passion and proficiency for travel.

When you have a clear focus like that, all of your actions drive you toward your end goal. Erik knew he didn't fit the typical nine-to-five job structure. He wanted to travel the world, and that's what he worked toward. He wasn't tempted to start a prank channel or do comedy sketches, because those things didn't drive him toward his end goal.

Now, he works with tour companies in countries all over the world, gets sponsored by Fortune 500 companies, and thrives as an influencer in the travel vlogger space. And his growth hasn't stopped. Since the first edition of this book, he has grown to over 1.7 million subscribers, worked with brands such as American Airlines and Google, and collaborated with Ryan Serhant of Bravo's *Million Dollar Listing*. That's the power of clarifying your content and staying committed and consistent. The YouTube revolution is growing at a faster rate than ever before!

Melanie Ham, who runs a quilting and crocheting channel, started out with the simple goal of making money from home while her husband was in the military. She was passionate about quilting and crocheting, and she had proficiency in them, though she'd never had any formal training. She decided to share what she knew online and grew an audience on YouTube. Now, she profits through YouTube advertising and selling her own digital products. The products she sells relate directly to her channel. Due to her clear focus, her end goal, and the intersection of the three Ps, Melanie is now earning a significant income for her family from YouTube.

Once you know the niche of your YouTube channel and the direction you want to go, you must answer two big questions. First, *who* is your target audience? Second, *what* will you offer them?

WHO IS YOUR TARGET AUDIENCE?

Who is your content intended for? It's a mistake to say, "Everybody." In fact, that is a recipe for failure. If you try to reach everybody, you'll wind up reaching nobody. Target a specific group of people who share your interests, because they will engage with your content.

As in Erik Conover's case, your target audience might be people who love to watch travel vlogs. Those same people probably might not jump over to Melanie Ham's channel and watch tutorials on quilting. Both Erik and Melanie have a specific group of people they try to reach with every video they upload, which is what makes them both successful YouTubers.

When defining your target audience, ask yourself the following questions: How old are they? What are their hobbies? What are they interested in? Where do they come from? What groups or niche communities are they a part of? It sounds counterintuitive, but success on YouTube comes from a narrow focus. In fact, the smaller your target audience in the beginning, the faster you'll grow.

TEN QUESTIONS TO CLARIFY YOUR TARGET AUDIENCE

1. Are they female, male, or both?

2. How old are they? We recommend picking a range within five years of your own age.

3. What types of jobs or professions do they have?

4. What are their passions?

5. What are the top three websites they visit?

6. What are the top three Twitter, TikTok, Instagram, and/or Facebook pages they follow?

7. Who are the top three influencers they might watch on YouTube?

8. What is their social circumstance? (Married, single, kids, no kids, family, etc.)

9. What is their yearly income range?

10. What products or services might they spend their discretionary income on? (Books, digital products, hobby expenses, etc.)

WHAT WILL YOU OFFER THEM?

Once you've narrowed down your audience, you must decide what you're going to offer them. How often will you post videos? Once or twice a week? Once a month? Will you offer entertainment, education, inspiration, information, or motivation? Write your answers down on paper and think about them ahead of time.

If you had twenty seconds on an elevator to pitch your YouTube channel to a stranger, how would you pitch it? Tell them what they can expect, who the channel is for, why they should be interested, how it will add value to their life, and why it matters. Many YouTube channels never grow because their creators never take the time to define a target audience and come up with a clear purpose, value, or reason why people should care about their content.

Picture the person on the other side of your video. They go onto YouTube, open up a search query, and type something in. What are they looking for? What piece of content do they seek? What problem might they have that your YouTube channel could answer? Don't forget, YouTube is a search engine, first and foremost. You need to be clear in the questions you want to answer and the value you're giving the world. Putting yourself in the seat of the viewer will allow you to find the questions and *become* the answers.

SUCCESS STORIES

Benji started his food channel because he's absolutely obsessed with cooking. If he wasn't sharing that passion on YouTube, he would be sharing it somewhere else. He's completely self-taught and has no formal culinary training—he's never even worked at a restaurant—but he's been cooking for most of his life, so he has become quite proficient. He wanted to connect with other people who loved food and had a passion for cooking, and that's what inspired him to start his channel. Looking back, he's very glad he did, because his channel now has over 378,000 subscribers, and his recipe videos have been viewed over twenty-six million times.

To build his audience, he had to connect with others by creating content about popular recipes. He never officially classified himself as a "how-to" chef. Instead, he just started sharing great recipes, dove deeper into the food industry, and built his audience. Over time, he's managed to profit through advertising, brand deals, and more.

Beyond that, his YouTube channel has provided him with amazing opportunities and experiences that he never would have had otherwise. Not long ago, he had one of those unique experiences at the nicest restaurant in Seattle, Canlis. Because he has developed a food reputation on YouTube, the owner of the restaurant came to the table and invited Benji and his wife down into the wine cellar. There, they were allowed to saber a rare bottle of champagne and taste a rare scotch out of the barrel.

On another occasion, Benji was invited into the kitchen of a steakhouse to work on a legendary Montague Broiler. That's an experience normally reserved for famous chefs or Food Network stars.

It's not all about making money. You never know what opportunities, relationships, or experiences will come your way as a result of building your influence on YouTube. Beyond having clarity for your numbers, you should have clarity for the kind of lifestyle you want to create. Benji wanted a lifestyle built around his passion for food: free to shop, cook, and eat delicious food every day and make a living doing it.

Because Benji was both passionate and proficient, brands wanted to align with him to promote their products. He used this to his advantage, creating segments on his channel that directly correlated with sponsorships. For example, he has a segment titled "Tea Tuesday," where he talks about his favorite teas. This segment has resulted in tons of free tea being sent to him.

For almost two decades, Sean has worked in video production. He has worked with, purchased, and researched cameras in the process, developing real expertise. He's completely self-taught, but he discovered he has an ability to speak naturally and authoritatively about cameras and video. Because of this, he became a source of advice and solutions for people who didn't have hours to pour through manuals.

Sean turned his expertise into five-minute instructional videos on his YouTube channel *Think Media*. His aim was to help people find the best cameras and lighting and to teach video production. In the process, he managed to generate a full-time income using a range of revenue strategies, and today, *Think Media* has over 1.8 million subscribers and his videos have been viewed 150 million times.

Cassie and Ricci of the channel *ToThe9s* are a great example of YouTubers who have benefited from clarity. When they started their channel back in 2014, they, like so many, only had a general interest in becoming influencers on the platform, but they soon focused their content around their passion for fashion. Though they've uploaded many different types of content over the years, they've maintained that fashion focus.

Three hundred videos, thirty-nine million views, and 617,000 subscribers later, they've proved they are doing something right. In addition to making YouTube their full-time business, they also work with numerous fashion brands who sponsor their content. Recently, they partnered with Adidas Canada.

They have a fan-based Instagram account, @weareto-the9s, where they highlight photos submitted by their followers. By featuring fan content, they have been able to accrue over 57,000 followers on Instagram. Their laser focus and clarity in messaging has turned general viewers into raving fans.

When we first met Cassi and Ricci, their long-term goal was to travel for fashion. Their success has allowed them to achieve this goal through the support of hundreds of thousands of fans around the world. At this point, they might be tempted to try something different, to chase trends outside of fashion, but they maintain their clarity. Even their daily vlogs include picking out clothes and shopping at clothing stores.

Clarity is power, and a clear understanding of your end goal will help you reverse engineer the steps to get there. Once you know your end goal, define your audience, and set your focus, it's time to start your journey on YouTube by creating your channel and building a home for your content.

CHAPTER 3

• • •

CHANNEL: BUILDING A HOME FOR YOUR CONTENT

"You never get a second chance to make a first impression."

—WILL ROGERS

We both love parties. Who doesn't? There's nothing better than good food and spending time with family and friends. However, it can be stressful when you invite guests over for the first time because you want to make a good first impression. So, what do you do? You try to clean up any messes in the house, you decorate, and you make sure everything is ready to welcome your guests.

In the same way, your YouTube channel serves as the home for your content, so make sure it welcomes your guests and makes a good impression. The first step, of course, is creating your channel. Your YouTube channel is a lot like a website, which means it's something you can personalize, customize, and make your own.

Another great way to think about your YouTube channel is to liken it to a TV channel. If you love sports, you've got ESPN. If you love comedy, you've got Comedy Central. If you love music and entertainment, you have MTV. We encourage you to think of your videos as the shows on your channel. Just like most TV channels, your YouTube channel should have some big idea that can be translated into a cohesive brand.

Anytime someone watches one of your videos, they consider subscribing to the whole channel. That's the importance of your brand. Each video should give people a good idea of what the whole channel has to offer. The clearer the purpose and passion of your channel, the more likely you are to get subscribers.

TAKE YOUR FIRST STEPS

The cool thing about starting a YouTube channel is that it's completely free. All you need is a Gmail address. If you don't already have one, create one. Then sign up for your YouTube channel. It's that easy.

You'll have to choose a name for your channel. If you're promoting a personal brand or your individual proficiency, the channel name could be as simple as your first and last name. Many successful channels have done this. Another option is to give your channel a creative brand or business name. The more descriptive it is, the better, so consider including the topic of your channel as part of the name. That makes it clearer to your target audience.

For example, *Nerd Fitness* is a fitness channel geared toward gamers, geeks, and nerds. It does a great job of combining both the topic and the target audience in the name. *Epic Meal Time* creates outrageous videos of people consuming things like 20,000-calorie, supersized lasagnas. The name fits their content perfectly.

Stuck on creating a channel name? Check out this video from *Video Influencers*: TubeSecretsBook.com/NameIdeas.

It's a good idea to secure a website URL with your YouTube channel name, even if you don't use it right away. You could experience breakout success, so you want to have a URL ready to go. Similarly, make sure the social media handles with your channel name are available. If so, claim them in the beginning before anyone else does.

When we came up with the name Video Influencers, we checked to make sure the URL was available and purchased it. Then we went to Instagram, Twitter, and

Facebook, our main social media platforms, and secured our account name on those platforms as well.

What if your URL or social media handles of choice aren't available? Don't get stuck. It doesn't mean you shouldn't go with that channel name. Just pick the closest thing you can get and don't worry about it. For example, we couldn't get @VideoInfluencers as a Twitter handle because it was one character too long, so we chose @VideoInfluencer instead. It hasn't hurt our success, and it won't hurt yours. Claim the name as close to your channel name as possible, do it in the very beginning, and move on.

By protecting your name across your channel, website, and social media profiles, you protect yourself for future opportunities. You might even research a trademark. You're starting small, but someday, if your channel becomes huge, you might want to promote products and do many things that haven't even crossed your mind.

Because we believed Video Influencers would be big and we wanted to protect our brand, we bought our trademark before we did anything with our channel. That way, if someday we decided to have a clothing line or some other product, we would have the means to do so.

BECOME A STANDOUT

Now that you've created your channel and you've picked a name, you need to fill out a few key areas. First, select an avatar. That's the small, square image beside your channel name. If it's your personal channel, find a nice headshot. If it's a brand, you might use a logo. Whatever you choose, make it eye-catching, interesting, and clear. The second area is your YouTube cover art. This is a big banner at the top of your channel page, and it gives people their first impression of your content.

When someone lands on your channel page, you have, at most, five seconds to shape their opinion of you. Your cover art must grab their attention and create the right impression. Make sure it communicates who the channel is for, what it's about, and why it should matter to the viewer. As in life, you only get one chance to make a first impression, so make sure your cover image is strong.

A third area to fill out on your channel page is your social media accounts. YouTube makes it easy to link to all your active social media profiles, as well as your website. Fourth, fill out your "About" page. We recommend not only introducing who you are and what the channel is about, but also clearly articulating what people can expect from it, why it will help them, and what value it provides.

Sometimes, people get too "me" focused on their About

page. They write something like, "This channel is about me. It's about my thoughts, and I think you should subscribe." We don't recommend that kind of language. Use the word "you" more, so it reads something like this: "You can expect lighthearted videos, encouragement, livestreams, and entertainment." You can also connect an email account here so that businesses, brands, and other people can get in touch with you for collaborations. You never know what kind of opportunities will come your way as you build your influence on YouTube.

Fifth, you can create a video and select it in the YouTube Studio as your channel trailer, which will be the first video people see who haven't subscribed. You can either create a video introducing your channel and letting viewers know what to expect, or you can simply select one of the videos you've already created that will make the best first impression for new viewers. While you can get away with not creating a channel trailer, it's a good idea to at least select your best-performing video.

Bear in mind, the primary way you communicate the look, feel, and brand of your YouTube channel is your videos, your video thumbnails, and the playlists they are organized in. Don't worry about this too much if you're just starting, because you won't have many videos to organize. Eventually, you'll want to organize your videos into categories on the home page of your YouTube channel.

For example, on youtube.com/ThinkMediaTV, Sean and the *Think Media* team do product reviews and tutorials on cameras and video gear for creating content. Videos from the channel have been organized into categories like "Video Lighting for Beginners," "The Best Microphones for Video and Audio Tips," and "Cameras for Dummies: YouTube Camera Basics for Video." The thumbnails on each video are the strongest (and only) visual element driving the look and brand of the channel.

Consider brainstorming three categories or larger topics your videos could be grouped in and organized into playlists. Then, once you've posted your first few videos, your home page will start coming to life.

Optimizing your channel page in these ways makes the difference between being the Coca-Cola on the shelf or some generic cola brand. Go the extra mile. Spruce up your look so that, even if you have videos that are similar to other channels, your presentation is clear and stands out.

Remember, when someone lands on your channel page, you have five seconds to make a first impression. You won't regret taking a little extra time to make it look as nice as possible.

DON'T SWEAT IT (TOO MUCH)

In this chapter, we have encouraged you to think about your channel name and given tips for setting up your channel page. Ultimately, building your channel is about building your *brand*. While these tips and strategies are important, and we encourage you to do your best, don't get stuck at this point.

At the end of the day, your content is more important than your channel name or channel art. In the next chapter, we'll show you how to create powerful video content that reaches your ideal audience and builds your influence, so turn the page and let's continue our journey.

CHAPTER 4

. . .

CONTENT: CREATE LASTING IMPACT

"Content marketing is the only marketing left."

—SETH GODIN

Have you ever turned off a movie or TV show halfway through? We certainly have. Why did we do that? Because it didn't hold our interest. Have you ever stopped reading a book? We hope you don't stop reading this one, but the reason you'd stop reading is because it didn't hold your attention, or the information wasn't good, or you didn't find it inspiring or motivational.

The reality is, if content doesn't add value to our lives, we abandon it. We live in a world where we can quickly close one video and start another at the click of a button. Value should be your focus when creating any content, on

YouTube or any other platform. The value can be informational through news, entertaining through comedy, educational, or even connecting on a deeper, personal level through vlogging.

Beyond that, you can inspire and motivate. People go to YouTube with the expectation of receiving something. When you're wondering what sort of video to create, think about the kind of value you want to provide to people. If you aren't naturally talented, or don't look like a superstar, or aren't personable, the value you deliver trumps everything. YouTube has been a game-changer for so many ordinary people because it turns them into superstars through the value of the content they create.

DELIVERING VALUE

Great content is anything that adds value to a viewer's life, so ask yourself, "What kind of value are viewers getting?" We believe every piece of content should deliver at least one of the following:

NEWS AND INFORMATION

This would include channels presenting interesting facts, breaking news, the latest gossip stories, and world events. It also includes top ten channels with videos like "Top Ten Things to Do in Greece."

ENTERTAINMENT

This content causes viewers to laugh, to smile, to cry. It's sharable. It's fun. It's compelling.

EDUCATION

This content helps viewers solve a problem, become better at something, or learn a skill.

INSPIRATION AND MOTIVATION

Inspiration and motivation go hand in hand. These videos get the viewer pumped up and excited. They get people to think bigger or feel better about themselves. They add a boost to a viewer's week.

CONNECTION AND COMMUNITY

No matter what type of videos you create, you must provide your audience with a feeling of connection. Connecting to a community of people allows your viewers to feel like they're a part of something bigger than themselves.

CHOOSING YOUR CONTENT

What type of content do you most enjoy watching on YouTube? Maybe you're a food lover. Do you enjoy watching people eating, or do you prefer cooking shows? What do you value the most, and is it something you want to recreate?

Even better, is there some kind of content you don't see on YouTube, or you don't see being done well, that you would enjoy? It's perfectly fine to recreate what other people are doing, or to improve upon somebody else's content, but it's more powerful to create something new. Whatever you choose, make sure your content resonates with your experience, with your skills and talents, and with your personality. Getting to that sweet spot requires some self-awareness.

Play to your strengths. Are you more analytical and factual? Consider providing informative content. Have people told you that you have a natural talent for encouraging people and making them feel better? If so, consider finding a way to motivate and inspire people. Are you a connector who enjoys making people feel welcomed and included? Then focus on creating connection and community.

The best content creators do all of the above. A popular term on YouTube is "edutainment," and it refers to content that combines education and entertainment. Those who do it well are experiencing massive success. The best content creators inform, inspire, educate, entertain, and build a community all at once.

HOW OFTEN TO RELEASE NEW CONTENT

More is usually better on YouTube. The more frequent your uploads, the more attention your channel will get. However, consistency is even more important. Find a balance between uploading often and keeping your quality consistent. Make sure you're committed for the long haul.

In our interview with Ellie and Jared Mecham, family vloggers with over 1.6 million subscribers and 770 million views who have documented their journey with infertility and pregnancy, they shared with us a simple formula for success on YouTube based on the acronym CQC: Consistent Quality Content. A common element of YouTube success is posting quality content on a consistent basis.

If you plan on creating a platform and growing your brand on YouTube, we recommend posting at least one new video each week. If you can post more, and keep your quality high, we encourage you to do so, but we believe quality is more important than quantity. Every piece of content needs to have value for viewers.

If you upload a video every day for fifty-two days, but then you stop and don't upload anything for the rest of the year, that won't benefit you as much as uploading one video a week for fifty-two weeks. People get excited about becoming YouTubers and creating content, but then they get burned out. It's better to spread out your content over a longer period of time. That's when you start seeing real results.

Remember to think of your YouTube channel like a TV channel. Your favorite program airs once a week at a specific time, so the audience can depend on it. If you want to build loyalty, momentum, and trust between you and your audience, then you need to show up on a regular basis delivering the same value every time.

Like a TV show, weekly is the minimum. What do you suppose would happen if a popular TV show suddenly failed to air at the expected time on the expected day of the week? There would be outrage among the fans and a loss of trust. What if it happened more than once? The show would lose viewers permanently, as fans started to think, "Was the show canceled? Is it not on the air anymore?" When a TV show loses consistency, people forget about it and look for other content. The same is true on YouTube. To build true influence, income, and impact on YouTube, you must be consistent.

MAKING YOUR VIDEOS STAND OUT

We encourage you to spend time watching content from other successful YouTubers in your niche and writing down ideas. What do you like about their content? What do you not like about it? What ideas could you potentially apply to your own content? Also, it can be helpful to watch videos outside of your niche. Some of the best ideas come from unrelated subject matter.

Content value matters more than production value. The best camera in the world with the best-looking picture quality won't impact your audience unless the content is interesting. It doesn't matter how good your video looks if it's devoid of value. However, the production value is still important, so if your content is interesting, we also encourage you to level up your production value.

Make a list of things you'd like to upgrade and improve when it comes to your content. Do you want to get a new camera? Can you improve your lighting? Could you decorate your home, studio, or office, or your workplace studio in a better way to make your content more visually appealing? Let this be a guiding principle: always start with what you have and then work to improve it over time. That applies to both your content and your production quality.

It's not about your resources, it's about your *resourcefulness*.

If you've already built an audience, another tip for making your content stand out is to ask them for feedback. Viewers love to feel involved. Successful YouTubers evolve as they get feedback and learn from their community—hearing what's good, what's bad, what could be made better, and getting content ideas. Ask people to provide feedback in the comments. The YouTube Community tab is a feature you get once you have over five hundred subscribers, so you might even consider running a survey on your YouTube "community" tab or using a service like SurveyMonkey and sharing it on social media.

If you want to build a community, your content has to continually resonate with your fans, but you also have to actively connect with your community, so turn the page, because we're going to share with you our best tips for doing that.

Struggling to come up with ideas for your first few videos? We've got you covered! Check out the free tips at TubeSecretsBook.com/Ideas.

CHAPTER 5

. . .

COMMUNITY: ENGAGE WITH YOUR AUDIENCE

"The Internet is becoming the town square for the global village of tomorrow."

—BILL GATES

The essence of what makes a YouTube influencer different from a Hollywood influencer is the connection you have with your audience. Your relationship with the audience is key to building trust, and that trust is where you'll find opportunity.

We love going to the movies. Nothing beats a good movie, especially the ones where you can lay back, kick up your feet, and soak up the action, comedy, and thrills. However, YouTube doesn't work that way. Viewers aren't simply reclining in their sofas, absorbing content. Instead, they are leaning forward to engage in a two-way conversation. It's not enough to simply publish content on YouTube. You need to build a community.

A recent article from *The Verge* revealed that YouTube's primetime audience is bigger than the top ten TV shows *combined*.[20] Statistics from Google show that YouTube reaches more eighteen-to-forty-nine-year-olds than any cable network in the US. The former model of pushing content without conversation doesn't work with the current generation. You must create a community to thrive and grow.

FIND YOUR COMMUNITY

It's important to figure out who your community is. First, and most importantly, your community is composed of your YouTube subscribers. Every YouTuber wants to grow their subscriber base as much as possible. The more subscribers you have, the more attention your videos get. That's the primary way to get to the next level. In a way, people watching your videos is kind of like going on a date. If you can get them to subscribe, you've gone from the first date to a relationship. It means the viewer liked your content enough to stay regularly involved with you.

---

20   Ben Popper, "YouTube Says Its Primetime Audience Is Bigger than the Top TV Shows Combined," *The Verge*, May 6, 2016, https://www.theverge.com/2016/5/6/11608036/youtube-bigger-than-tv-brandcast-sia.

They want updates, they want connection, and they're willing to commit.

> **Power Tip:** YouTube allows people to turn on notifications for your channel, so encourage subscribers to become super subscribers by hitting that notification button. They will be informed every time you release a new video via an email and mobile notifications. The button looks like a bell, so if you can convince people to ring the bell, it's like going from the first date, to dating consistently, to getting engaged. In a business sense, getting married is the final step and would be if somebody becomes a customer of yours or invests with you at a deeper level.

If people follow you on the social media platforms connected to your YouTube channel, that creates another level of community. The people who are willing to do this are sold on your videos and want to continue receiving your content, but now they are also actively engaging in the conversation. Invite your viewers to follow you on social media and let them know which platforms you're most active on so they connect with you at a deeper level. If you can get them to do so, you are creating an audience that values the interaction, and that's huge for channel growth. That's why on platforms like Instagram, replying to people's comments and sharing their posts you're tagged on is so important.

What if your channel starts with zero subscribers? How can you build an audience from nothing? Well, technically, everybody starts at zero, so don't feel discouraged. First, don't overthink it. Just post your first video. You'll never feel ready, so punch fear in the face and press record.

Second, commit to posting at least thirty to fifty videos before you get overly critical about how many views you're getting or your subscriber growth. We know that sounds daunting, but it takes time to trigger the YouTube algorithm. We want to set realistic expectations for when you can expect to see some momentum. Remember, your channel will grow one video at a time, one video *view* at a time, and one subscriber at a time. Pace yourself—this is a marathon, not a sprint.

Third, keep reading because you're going to learn powerful tips and strategies on how to grow your channel faster in the second part of this book. However, if you want some quick strategies to jumpstart your growth, watch this video: TubeSecretsBook.com/StartFromZero.

CONTINUE TO BUILD YOUR COMMUNITY

After uploading content on YouTube, the best way to build your community is asking people to subscribe. Always remind your viewers to subscribe to your channel. Many content creators make the mistake of assuming that viewers know about subscribing, but the truth is, many viewers either don't know or don't think about it. The creators who ask people to subscribe in every video tend to have larger audiences.

Give viewers a good reason to subscribe. Don't just annoy them with constant requests. A huge mistake we see You-Tubers make is sounding desperate, begging people to subscribe instead of leading with value. A good way to encourage subscribers might sound like this, "If you have gotten value from this video, don't forget to subscribe, so you never miss one of my brand-new weekly recipe videos." Then you're not just pleading for subscribers but providing a compelling reason.

Make sure the video is valuable for viewers because people appreciate what you do for them. Also, make sure your call to action tells them what they'll get out of subscribing. It might sound something like the following: "Subscribe to *Video Influencers* for more interviews just like this one about how to grow your YouTube channel." Provide an incentive or a value proposition so people know what kind of community you're building.

Another powerful way to build community is by encouraging people to leave comments on your videos. When they do leave a comment, always take the time to respond, especially when you're just getting started. On *Video Influencers*, we provide a question of the day for each video and invite people to answer in the comments. Doing this repeatedly over time has built an engaged community on our YouTube channel.

Engagement with your audience through comments creates a deeper connection with viewers. Remember, a real person is on the other side of their device taking the time to leave a comment on your video. Responding to those comments in a meaningful, grateful, and helpful way is important for building a strong, positive reputation and a lasting brand on YouTube.

Conversation sets YouTube apart from traditional media like television or movies. Viewers can provide direct feedback and opinions about every video. They can critique, compliment, and criticize—that's the beauty of it. Respond to everything the community throws at you, so you can build your tribe.

But YouTube comments alone aren't enough. Go above and beyond to engage with people on other social media platforms. We make it a goal to respond to every comment, tweet, Facebook message, or Instagram direct message (DM). As your platform grows, this becomes more challenging, but a commitment to do this in the early stages of your channel is key. It's the difference between those who succeed at building a community and those who do not.

Yes, it's hard, and it takes a lot of time. We know you're

busy, but you should never be too busy for your fans. No YouTube channel succeeds without regular viewers, so we believe every creator should commit to connecting with their community in every way possible.

NAME YOUR COMMUNITY

Many of the top YouTubers have created a community name for their fans. The biggest YouTuber, PewDiePie, creates gaming videos and calls his fans "bros." The family vlogging channel *SacconeJolys* calls their viewers "friendliest friends." We call our community "influencers." Personal brands like Gary Vaynerchuk call their audience "Vayniacs" and Tina Singh (Lilly Singh's sister) calls her mom army of followers "Marmy." Emily Baker is a trial attorney turned full-time YouTuber who has built a passionate community who call themselves "the Law Nerds." Creating a community name allows fans and superfans to affiliate, self-declare, and self-align with a community and tribe.

CREATE DEEP CONNECTIONS

If you want to connect with viewers at a deeper level, you can message them directly or reply to them in text, in video, or in audio. For example, Sean often replies on Twitter with a Twitter video when someone reaches out, and the receiver is usually shocked and amazed. On the other hand, Benji has discovered that replying to Instagram DMs with a video response is a powerful way of building a bond. The opportunity to do this exists on Facebook, Instagram, Twitter, or your favorite social media platform. Viewers value this kind of direct interaction as much as, if not more than, your actual video content.

We often spend thirty to sixty seconds in a video simply thanking or acknowledging specific viewers or answering questions from our community. When we do that, especially when we name names, people feel encouraged, surprised, and happy to see that we care enough to take the time to speak to them. A great example of someone who makes deep connections with his fans is Justin Khoe. His mission is to help people on their journey of faith and understanding the Bible. During the initial growth of his channel, he always made time in his schedule to reply to every email, and to make phone calls and Skype calls with anybody who asked.

Besides creating extraordinarily deep relationships with people, he also receives helpful feedback on his channel. He uses that feedback to learn more about his community and create better content. Due to his diligence in becoming an active member of his community, he was able to turn YouTube into a full-time career. From there, he built his income through crowdfunding and audience support in a little over a year.

Depth matters. Always look for ways you can create meaningful connections with your community. It always pays off in the long run. When you create and nurture your community, you build trust. That trust and engagement will enable you to create consistent income through committed viewers.

BECOME A JUDY

Benji's wife, Judy of *It's Judy Time*, was the first YouTube success story we ever observed. She has millions of subscribers, thousands of videos, over a billion video views, and has been on YouTube for over ten years. She started with makeup videos, but now she also sells her own products, works with YouTube directly, and has experienced amazing success.

When people ask us how she became so famous and successful, we say that, outside of her content, the most significant contributing factor to her success is the trust she's built with her viewers. In the first few years of her YouTube career, when she was relatively unknown, she only spent half of her time creating content. The other half she spent engaging with her audience. In fact, every day, from 10 p.m. until two or three in the morning, she engaged with her audience directly.

At the time, the people she responded to weren't even

committed fans. They were viewers leaving comments, tweeting, or responding to her blog posts. Judy spent tons of time answering questions, continuing conversations on topics from her videos, and building community before she even knew what community was. The reason she stands apart from other creators today is because she valued her viewers as much as, if not more than, her own content.

As an example of how committed and loyal Judy's fan base is, almost every time she launches a new product online, it sells out, in many cases on the first day. Additionally, even after changing her niche, leaving her beauty channel, and creating 3,600 vlog episodes, she still consistently gets 100,000 to 200,000 views every upload because of the loyalty of her viewers.

Ten years into her YouTube career, Judy has become one of the most trusted influencers in her space, and that trust is the essence of what makes a YouTube creator different from other kinds of celebrities. That trust lays a foundation for almost every opportunity you can receive.

DEVELOP TRUE FANS

From the very first video you upload, begin creating your community through engagement. You don't need a large audience to build a full-time business or personal brand on

YouTube; you just need an engaged audience of true fans. Chris Pirillo, founder of the event in Seattle, Washington, called VloggerFair, said, "The size of the community doesn't matter as much as the depth of the connections with them."

This idea is explained further in the famous article by Kevin Kelly that says, "To be a successful creator, you do not need millions of dollars or millions of customers, millions of clients or millions of fans. To make a living as a craftsperson, photographer, musician, designer, author, animator, app maker, entrepreneur, or inventor, you only need a thousand true fans."[21]

Here's the actual math, according to Kelly. You have to create enough value that you can earn, on average, one hundred dollars of profit a year from each fan. You can do this by using the monetization strategies we offer in this book. Remember, it's always easier to go deeper with the fans you already have than to find or grow new fans. Create a direct relationship with them, so that they are paying you directly. That way, you keep the full one hundred dollars from each fan. Then, you only need one thousand of them to earn $100,000 per year. That's a great living for most people.

---

21   Kevin Kelly, "1,000 True Fans," The Technium, accessed March 5, 2022, https://kk.org/thetechnium/1000-true-fans/.

Gaining a thousand true fans is much easier than aiming for a million, especially when you're just starting out. If you can add just one new fan a day, you can get to a thousand in a few years.

Build your community of true fans by generating trust with your viewers. Trust and engagement enable you to create a consistent income. In the next chapter, we'll show you how you can monetize your content and turn your passion into profit and your creativity into a career.

CHAPTER 6

. . .

CASH: MONETIZE YOUR CONTENT

"Chase the vision, not the money, and the money will end up following you."

—TONY HSIEH, FORMER ZAPPOS CEO

Some people think talking about money is taboo. The way we're raised tends to shape our emotions and mindset when it comes to money. However, one thing is for sure: money follows and fuels mission.

We encourage you to stay grounded in your reason, mission, and motivation for building your influence on YouTube. Whether your purpose was to impact people around the world, build a community, entertain and inspire, or provide for yourself and your family, you need to keep that reason at the forefront of your mind as you adventure further into the process.

To serve your mission and vision at the highest level, you need resources. More specifically, you need money. With money, you have more freedom with your content and production quality. You can hire a team and support others, whether employees, assistants, or a charity you love. With money, you can maximize your effectiveness in the world.

MONETIZING ON YOUTUBE

We want to share with you ten ways to build your income on YouTube, but we advise you to never chase the money. That's a recipe for frustration. Chase your focus, your mission, your passion, and your purpose, and allow money and income to stem from that. This chapter isn't meant to define the *only* ways to make money. There are far more ways to generate a good income than we could possibly cover in a single book, so instead, we will provide you with a few key monetization strategies and ideas.

ADSENSE

The first and most widely understood way of making money on YouTube is with the AdSense program. Once your YouTube channel has over one thousand subscribers and four thousand hours of watch time, it will be eligible for revenue sharing through the AdSense program. This gives YouTube permission to play ads on your video, and a portion of the ad revenue is granted to you.

The amount of money you can make from AdSense varies. As a typical rule of thumb, creators in the US are paid an average of two dollars per one thousand views. Therefore, if you want to make $2,000 per month from YouTube content, you would need one million views per month. That's no easy feat, especially on a consistent basis. When you're first starting out, it may not be enough, but if you stay consistent, it can turn into a significant source of income over the long term, as it has for countless YouTube creators.

The AdSense strategy is best for prank, comedy, news, vlog, and entertainment channels, which tend to garner a large number of views. Content trying to go viral is a prime example. Most high-view channels fall into the entertainment category, but education channels can crush it with AdSense as well. Graham Stephan, who shares advice on personal finance, investing, and real estate, revealed that monetizing the videos on his three YouTube channels enabled him to earn over $1.8 million in 2020. He also earns income from the additional strategies mentioned in this chapter. Combined, this has taken his yearly income to over $4 million.[22]

22 Graham Stephan, "How Much I Make with 2 Million Subscribers," YouTube video, 15:13, https://youtu.be/9vpwTxALZAs.

While Graham's results are certainly extraordinary, what if you managed to achieve just 10 percent of his success? Ten percent of his yearly revenue would mean you're earning over $400,000. Just 1 percent would be over $40,000. The US Census Bureau lists the annual real median personal income at $35,977 in 2019.[23] So, you might not become a millionaire, but it's more practical than ever to earn a full-time living from creating content on YouTube.

Even when you're just starting, long before you get approved for the YouTube Partner Program, there are many ways to earn money from YouTube.

One of the reasons why YouTube is significant as a platform is because of AdSense. No other platform offers such a practical source of passive income as AdSense YouTube revenue. You don't have to become a businessperson. You just create the content, and YouTube does all the hard work of bringing the ad revenue to you!

AFFILIATE MARKETING

With affiliate marketing, you earn a commission by promoting a company's products. The process is simple: find a product you like, promote it, and earn a piece of the profit

---

23   Wikipedia, s.v., "Personal Income in the United States," accessed July 8, 2021, https:// en.wikipedia.org/wiki/Personal_income_in_the_United_States.

for each sale. All you have to do is find a company with an affiliate program. The most common affiliate program is Amazon Associates, which you can join by applying online. Once approved, you can create your own links to Amazon products, and any time a viewer clicks on a link, you receive a percentage of the product's price, which could be anywhere between 1 to 10 percent.

As you can imagine, this income adds up quickly, as long as you work to increase the number of people clicking on your links. Affiliate marketing is relevant for any type of YouTube channel, but it works especially well for beauty, fashion, health, finance, tech, and review channels. That's because these kinds of channels tend to discuss specific products, services, and software. If there's a product related to your niche—physical, digital, service, or live event—there may be an affiliate program for it.

Even with a relatively small audience, you could eventually build a six-figure income from affiliate marketing. Sean has worked with cameras for years, so outside of *Video Influencers*, he started a channel called *Think Media*, where he advises people on the best cameras and equipment for filming. Affiliate links are helpful in this circumstance because he regularly reviews products, many of which he promotes and provides links to. Sean's first commission check from Amazon in 2010 was for a measly $2.12, but with consistency, patience, and getting 1 percent better on every video, his momentum started to build.

By 2016, Sean was generating a six-figure annual income through affiliate marketing, and today he earns as much as $40,000 a month from Amazon alone. CNBC recently covered his story in a ten-minute mini-documentary.[24] Amazon isn't the only affiliate program out there. Many different retail stores have programs you can apply for, including Target, Walmart, Kohl's, Sephora, Bass Pro Shops, Home Depot, and Nordstrom. The possibilities are almost endless for affiliate marketing. Whatever the nature of your channel, this is one source of income that is worth investigating.

YOUR OWN PRODUCT OR SERVICE

Another way to monetize your YouTube channel is to create a product or service. The benefit of selling your own product is that you don't make only a small percentage of the revenue. Instead, the full profit belongs to you. Many YouTubers have created their own lines of merchandise, such as T-shirts, coffee mugs, hats, and other apparel. Websites like Merch.Amazon.com have made creating your own merchandise easier than ever. Teespring.com now

---

24 Katie Schoolov and Erin Black, "This YouTube Product Reviewer Made Nearly $40,000 in April from Sending Viewers to Buy Products on Amazon," CNBC, June 3, 2020, https://www.cnbc.com/2020/06/03/youtube-reviewer-sean-cannell-made-40000-in-april-from-amazon.html.

integrates directly with YouTube, allowing you to create a "merch shelf" on the page below your videos. With their easy-to-use tool, you can create T-shirts, coffee mugs, posters, and more that viewers of your channel can purchase.

However, your products don't have to stop at apparel and coffee mugs. You can also create digital products, such as educational services, online courses, or ebooks.

Melanie Ham, who we interviewed on *Video Influencers*, has a crafting and DIY channel. She gives away tons of free videos, while also offering paid digital training videos on the side that go more in-depth. You can turn any knowledge you have into a digital product and offer it to your audience. You can even offer consulting or coaching, especially if it's relevant for your niche and vision.

We've seen YouTubers with small audiences make six-figure incomes from this strategy because they offer valuable, inexpensive premium content alongside their free videos. As you gain fans who want to connect with you on a deeper level, your products or services are the deeper level you can provide. It builds up your community and your connection with your fans.

FREE PRODUCT TRADE

A dollar saved is a dollar earned. Often, in the pursuit of

monetization, people forget that by saving in one place, they can spend in another. You can find brands, companies, or businesses that will send you free products in exchange for a review or promotion.

When Benji first started on YouTube with his then-fiancée Judy, he wasn't doing well financially. He needed to pay for their upcoming wedding, so he asked Sean to help him create a wedding series. Together, we created episodes around popular topics on wedding planning and reached out to brands we thought would want to sponsor us, such as bridal wear companies. For example, we created an episode around Judy trying on her wedding dress for the first time. The dress itself was provided by a wedding dress company, and in exchange for the free dress, we featured it in that episode.

The wedding series ultimately resulted in ten episodes that built up to the wedding and included the ceremony itself. Many of the episodes were sponsored through free products, and some episodes also received monetary sponsorship.

Though the whole series wasn't fully a paid sponsorship, it was a dollar saved where we would have spent. Your audience doesn't need to be especially large to take advantage of free product trades like this, but it helps if your audience is focused. Miguel, who is part of the Video Influencers community, launched a channel sharing tips on music recording. He and his wife are musicians. They put out songs and extended plays (EPs), and he wanted to launch a channel to help other people do the same. Because his channel is focused, he received over $7,000 worth of free products and software while he was still under 500 subscribers. Brands love to work with influencers who can prove their audience is aligned with the company's own target market, even if that market is small.

Whether you're a full-time YouTuber with one hundred thousand subscribers or you're new with less than one thousand, getting free products is as simple as reaching out through social media, sending an email, or even picking up the phone and asking. You will be surprised at how many companies will say yes. Every time you succeed at trading content for a product, you learn and get better at it, attracting more opportunities.

Often, the value you can offer a business, especially a smaller or local business like a restaurant, is the video you can produce for them. It might cost a business from a few hundred to a few thousand dollars to produce a professional quality video. As a creator, you can provide this for free in exchange for something from the business.

We know a YouTuber who loves food and travel. We advised him to use this technique to his advantage, even though he had almost no followers on his channel at the time. He went to a local restaurant and offered to produce a quality video for them that they could use on their website in exchange for a free meal. They took him up on the offer. His story isn't unique. This kind of exchange happens all the time. For companies, there's intrinsic value in these kinds of videos, even when the videos garner only a few views, so this is something you can get into when you're just starting out.

YOUR EXISTING BUSINESS

People tend to focus on monetizing solely within the YouTube environment. However, YouTube can also be used as an external arm and outreach for an existing business. Let's say you own a brick-and-mortar store. Your revenue comes almost exclusively from the store, but you could use a YouTube channel to produce content that promotes the business and expands your reach globally. Instead of making money directly from the videos, you're attracting people to the store, where the real revenue is generated. In addition to creating awareness about your local business, you can expand your reach online by setting up an e-commerce store or adding the additional revenue streams listed in this chapter.

When Benji rebuilt his real estate business, he decided to start a channel, *HomeDealzTV*, answering frequently asked real estate questions. He took the top questions people ask realtors, such as how to buy a house, how to price a house, and how to find a good agent, and provided the answers in a simple but compelling way. Even though the audience for this channel was relatively small, through this he delivered value to his local network, attracted clients, and turned his business around. He went from doing fewer than ten property deals a year to over a hundred, all because of a simple idea of giving value through a YouTube channel.

Remember, when it comes to monetization, YouTube is primarily a means of communication. At one time, it made sense to go door-to-door selling products and services in local neighborhoods, because that was the most direct means of communication. Now, YouTube offers the digital means to do the same thing on a much broader scale. We believe every smart business owner and brand should leverage tools like YouTube to expand their reach and revenue online.

If you're a current business owner, ask yourself what kind of value you could deliver through video for your potential clients or customers. Are there questions you could answer? Tips or advice you could provide? When you create value for viewers, you drive people back to your business.

CROWDFUNDING

Crowdfunding is the practice of funding a project or venture by raising small amounts of money from a large number of people, typically via internet sites like Kickstarter, Indiegogo, Patreon, and GoFundMe. On YouTube, Patreon is the top choice, widely used by many popular channels because it encourages regular support.

With Patreon, you ask people to pledge a certain amount of money, usually on a month-to-month basis, and offer specific rewards for varying levels of support. These rewards could be Q&A videos that only supporters can view, mentioning their names in the end credits of one of your videos, or any number of creative incentives to add value back to the audience.

Justin Khoe built influence, trust, and a relationship with his audience for about a year before starting a Patreon page. More than sixty people have committed to supporting his channel monthly through Patreon, giving him enough money to turn his YouTube mission into a full-time job.

Philip DeFranco runs a popular news channel on YouTube with a huge subscriber base. He supports his YouTube goals through AdSense. However, when YouTube made some changes to their ad policies, most of his content was labeled as "not advertiser friendly," eliminating most of the AdSense income from his YouTube videos overnight. He responded by launching a Patreon account, and over thirteen thousand people signed up to support him in his vision for creating a progressive news and entertainment network. Viewers can support his channel for as little as five dollars a month or as much as $1,000. If all of those supporters were only at the five-dollar level, that still comes out to over $65,000 in monthly support.

YouTube recently added the ability for fans to support you monthly through channel memberships. Ben Azadi from *Keto Kamp* uses this feature to give his community exclusive content. For $6.99 a month, a viewer can sign up to gain access to monthly Q&A sessions with Ben, discounted merchandise, a downloadable welcome bundle, and loyalty badges. YouTube keeps 30 percent of the monthly revenue generated from channel membership, and you get to keep the other 70 percent.

Crowdfunding disrupts the typical model of how things are done. In the past, people depended on the approval and support of the higher-ups and gatekeepers, yet crowdfunding empowers creators to support their vision and mission directly from the people who benefit from it the most.

We recommend building your influence before focusing on building an income. Launching something like a crowdfunding initiative before you have a crowd will more than likely fail. Building trust and loyalty with viewers is key to success in crowdfunding and most other money-making endeavors.

EVENTS

Events provide another way of monetizing your YouTube content. These events can happen live and in-person, or you can host them online. They can be free or require an admission charge, though it's far easier to invite people to a paid event once you've built a large audience.

A practical example would be a live performance. If you love a particular band or musician, buy their music on iTunes, listen to them on Spotify, and watch their videos on YouTube, the next step is to see them live. You'll pay a decent amount of money to attend that live performance, because you love their music. The same applies to you as an influencer on YouTube. If you're providing tons of value to your viewers, they will become fans, and they'll gladly buy tickets to see you at a live event.

A friend of ours, Daniel Eisenman, began hosting an event called International Tribe Design even when his audience was still fairly small. He took the trust and influence he'd built online to create events and meetups at unique locations around the world. Some of his fans gladly pay upwards of $2,000 just to attend these events. As a result of his popularity and success, Daniel has been able to visit exotic destinations, travel the world, and enjoy a lifestyle that most people only dream about, because he built his influence with online video first and then promoted live events to his audience.

In 2018, Sean and the *Think Media* team created an annual event called *Grow with Video Live*. While it is typically held in person in Las Vegas, during the global pandemic, it pivoted to an online event. The power of this event comes from creating connections and learning opportunities whether through in-person networking parties or online meetups using Zoom.

As we mentioned, paid events don't need to be physical meetups. You can also host a paid online event or summit where you gather a group of speakers who share their knowledge and experience about your particular niche. Viewers who care enough about the topic will gladly pay for the opportunity to hear expert speakers.

BRAND SPONSORSHIPS

Sponsorships, also called "brand deals" in the YouTube community, are a form of monetization that has become extremely popular on YouTube, especially for the bigger influencers. It works similarly to the free product trade we discussed earlier, with the added perk that companies pay real money in exchange for product promotions.

For example, if your YouTube channel does toy reviews, a toy company might reach out to you with an offer to work together. In exchange for bringing awareness to their company's products, you get paid a generous amount.

Brand sponsorships happen at many different levels. You can initiate them by reaching out to a brand yourself. However, some YouTubers work with agents who connect them with relevant brands. There are also online marketplaces for brand sponsorships such as AspireIQ. Signing up for AspireIQ is free, and you can get started with as few as three thousand subscribers.

Let's say you have a tech channel and you use AspireIQ to discover a headphone company that wants to work with influencers. You send them a proposal or connect directly through chat. From there, you can discuss potential trade or paid sponsorships. AspireIQ doesn't even take a percentage of the deal, and you get paid immediately from the brand through PayPal once you finish the deliverables. Your obligation might be as easy as wearing the headphone in your videos.

Eight months after Heather Torres started her homeschooling channel, it had grown to over 2,500 subscribers. She'd only posted fifteen videos, but she emailed the company that she purchased her curriculum from and inquired about the possibility of doing a collaboration. The company was mystified. They had no experience with YouTube branding deals, so she explained the possibilities and what a brand deal might look like. Eventually, they came to an agreement.

In that deal, the company gave her all of the curriculum for free, a value of over $800, and paid her $300 for each video talking about her experience with it. On top of that, they also set up an affiliate deal to give Heather a 10 percent commission for anyone who signed up for and purchased the curriculum through her channel links. The money generated from the video views and affiliate sales alone was enough to purchase brand new iPads for her kids.

Heather's experience proves that you don't have to be a large-scale YouTuber to take advantage of brand deals. As long as you have focused content, you might be able to generate interest with related companies.

In fact, companies call YouTubers like Heather *micro-influencers*. According to *Forbes* magazine, 82 percent of viewers are likely to follow a micro-influencer's rec-ommendations, which proves companies don't need to rely on huge channels to advocate for their brands.[25] We encourage you to consider which brands you want to collaborate with so you can start using brand deals to build your income.

Since the beginning of Benji's YouTube journey, brand sponsorship has been a significant part of his and his wife's business. When they first started, they charged less than one hundred dollars per promotion. However, over time brand deals led to a seven-figure annual business model for them.

After 2020, the need that brands have for the influence of these creators has grown significantly. For both micro- and mega-influencers, brand deals are more lucrative than ever.

For more information on getting sponsored, check out TubeSecretsBook.com/BrandDeals.

LICENSED CONTENT

Rather than creating their own videos, many companies are willing to pay YouTubers to license their content. Sometimes, the intrinsic value of your video has little to

---

25 Rafael Schwarz, "Is Smaller Better in Influencer Marketing?" *Forbes*, July 24, 2020, https://www.forbes.com/sites/forbescommunicationscouncil/2020/07/24/is-smaller-better-in-influencer-marketing.

do with your popularity and more to do with the content itself. In other words, the nature of a video sometimes has value on its own, separate from your channel. Various media companies can take and use it for their own purposes, paying you a licensing fee to do so.

Travel vloggers who create videos about interesting and exotic locations often work with local travel boards in various countries, licensing or selling the stock footage they shoot. Travel boards then use that footage in their own marketing and promotions.

Other influencers build their income by uploading their footage to stock video websites like istockphoto.com, VideoHive.net, or Shutterstock.com. Stock video marketplaces give creators another income opportunity by making it easy to license their content.

As you grow your authority, your influence, and the value of your brand, your face, image, likeness, and reputation also begin to acquire value to media outlets. Benji and his wife have often been able to double or triple their brand deal rates because of the licensing opportunities within their agreements when working with brands.

SPEAKING ENGAGEMENTS

A final way to build income and monetize your content

on YouTube that we want to share in this book is through speaking engagements. If you've built enough influence and authority around a topic, you become a valuable candidate for speaking at industry events, conferences, conventions, and even local events. Sean, for example, travels all over the country and even internationally, earning thousands of dollars in speaking fees. Amy Landino, a marketing and business coach, has leveraged her YouTube influence into ten to twenty paid speaking gigs a year at corporate events. Amy has a strong core audience on YouTube, but she's not a huge YouTuber. Despite this, she has created a significant income for herself. If you build your influence in a specific niche, you can use that influence to open the door to many speaking opportunities.

JP Sears, noted speaker, coach, and consultant, serves as an interesting case study. When he created his character Ultra Spiritual JP a couple of years ago, the videos quickly went viral. As a result, he received many requests to speak in character at events. In fact, he received so many requests that he got overwhelmed, but this drove up his speaking fee. As if that wasn't enough, his popularity and fan growth led to comedy shows across the country that have multiple events per location.

Building your personal brand on YouTube is powerful! Since the first edition of *YouTube Secrets*, we have been invited to speak at some of the biggest video marketing, business, and personal development events in the world.

Not only will YouTube continue to add new ways to earn money, but the strategies described in this chapter are only the tip of the iceberg when it comes to earning money with YouTube.

To learn the best and most current methods for making money with YouTube, watch our free YouTube monetization web class at TubeSecretsBook.com/FreeClass.

BEGINNER MISTAKES

When it comes to monetization, the biggest mistake we see creators make is focusing on income first instead of influence. Remember, influence must always come first, and it's impossible to build influence without adding value, creating a connection, starting a relationship, and ultimately building trust with people.

While we all know exceptions to this rule—people who make quick money by being dishonest or taking short-cuts—those people never last, and they never create legacies. On *Video Influencers*, we didn't turn on YouTube ads for over a year and a half, because we didn't want to hinder long-term audience growth with a shortsighted focus on making money.

Today, that is no longer an option because YouTube now runs ads on any video they choose.[26] However, your mentality should be the same. Influence comes first; income comes second. Add massive value and build trust before trying to monetize your audience.

Depending on your financial situation, you might need to start making money sooner than that. However, we don't recommend starting on YouTube out of desperation. You must have the determination and willingness to treat YouTube as a marathon and not a sprint. We wanted to build trust with people, and we knew those YouTube ads would not add up to significant income early on. Our first priority was modeling influence, then building a community, and finally, last of all, flipping the switch on monetization.

In one of our *Video Influencers* interviews, Lewis Howes, creator of one of the top podcasts on iTunes, *The School of Greatness*, reveals that he ran his podcast for two years before he added sponsors and other monetization opportunities.

Focus on building your influence, stay patient and persistent, and income will follow. Remember, money follows mission.

---

26   John Koetsier, "YouTube Will Now Show Ads On All Videos Even if Creators Don't Want Them," *Forbes*, November 18, 2020, https://www.forbes.com/sites/johnkoetsier/2020/11/18/youtube-will-now-show-ads-on-all-videos-even-if-creators-dont-want-them/.

A second mistake we see creators make is letting the monetization opportunity overshadow what's good for the audience. If a brand wants to promote their product on your channel because of your authority, trust, and large audience, make sure their product is appropriate for your audience. Even if they're offering a lot of money, don't agree to it if the monetization deal doesn't provide relevant, meaningful content for your loyal viewers. Otherwise, you will hurt your channel and lose their trust.

If you have a beauty channel where you provide makeup and hair care tips, and an electronics company approaches you to promote their TVs, it's not a good deal. If you agree to it, you will damage the integrity of your channel, because your viewers look to you for beauty tips.

As social media expert and *New York Times* bestselling author Gary Vaynerchuk says, "Doing the right thing is always the right thing." When monetization opportunities come your way, always put your audience first.

PICKING A STARTING POINT

Ask yourself, are you a coach or a teacher? Are you somebody who shares ideas or opinions? Are you someone who entertains? Figuring out your role in regard to your viewers helps you determine which monetization strategies work best for you.

For example, if you're a teacher, then having a digital product to teach additional techniques and skills might make more sense for you than doing a brand deal. If you entertain people through lifestyle vlogs, and you've grown an audience that likes and trusts you, then a brand sponsorship makes sense.

When picking a monetization option to start with, we recommend trying a few and narrowing it down through trial and error. Through experimentation, you will discover which method fits best with your brand, message, mission, and values. Turning on YouTube ads is the simplest way to start monetizing, but with a low number of views, it won't produce much income. Even so, it's a starting point. Affiliate marketing might be a better starting point, because you don't have to create any products yourself. All you do is make recommendations and get paid.

Some people do all the above. Individual forms of monetization might not make a lot of money, but by combining them all, some YouTubers manage to create significant income. Just as financial advisors recommend diversifying your portfolio, we recommend you diversify your income streams. That way, if something should dramatically change, like it did for Philip DeFranco, all of your eggs are not in one basket, and you have other income streams to lean on.

Whatever you decide to do, remember that the value in your videos comes first. Consistently delivering value must be your primary focus, no matter the monetization opportunities that come your way. Next, we'll take a closer look at how you can create consistency.

CHAPTER 7

. . .

CONSISTENCY: HUSTLE YOUR WAY TO SUCCESS

"Rome wasn't built in a day."

—JOHN HEYWOOD

You've probably heard that old adage. Well, it's true of more than just Rome. It always takes time to build something great.

Think about it. People spend years trying to master a skill, craft, or hobby. YouTube is no different. How was Rome built? Did people stand around doing nothing, waiting for the empire to appear? No, they laid down bricks every single day. The same goes for your YouTube channel. It's easy to focus on your YouTube empire and overlook the daily work of creating and uploading videos.

The brick-laying system is more important than the whole. Remember, the key to building momentum on YouTube is posting consistent strategic-quality content over time. In this chapter, we want to share with you some systems and principles that will help you continue to lay the bricks of YouTube success on your way to building an empire.

COMMITTING TO CONSISTENCY

The key to consistency on YouTube is to just show up. In business, those who show up are those who succeed. On YouTube, it's important to do so for a number of reasons.

- First, when you create consistent videos, it's like hanging out with a friend. The more often you hang out, the closer you get to that friend.
- Second, as you keep posting and observing the results, you learn more about the platform and the ever-changing YouTube algorithm, both of which are vital to channel growth. Consistency is more than getting content out there. It's about learning the process that creates success.
- Third, by showing up consistently, you get regular feedback from the audience that helps you improve your content.
- Fourth, you might feel overwhelmed with how many things you have to learn, but practice makes progress. The more videos you film, the better you get at camera

work. The more videos you edit, the better you get at editing.

Dale Carnegie said, "Learning is an active process. We learn by doing. Only knowledge that is used sticks in your mind."

Creating a schedule is imperative. That way people know when to expect your videos. Also, YouTube rewards consistent channels by pushing them higher in the search and recommended lists. Don't forget, as a business, YouTube generates revenue by selling ads on videos. Therefore, when you create consistent quality content, you position yourself for YouTube to promote your videos to a wider audience. They love to reward consistency.

Creating regular videos is hard work, but the harder you work, the luckier you get. When you post consistently, you put more opportunities into the world, more hooks in the sea, for people to find and discover you. You never know which video might become the video that opens up the door to success. Some of that is up to chance, but you can stack the deck in your favor by uploading more often.

For example, we are both full-time creators for our own channels and businesses, but when we started *Video Influencers*, we wanted to commit to one upload per week for the sake of consistency. It wasn't glamorous. Actually, it was a grind. Some of the videos perform better than others, but that weekly discipline has paid off in unexpected ways. In 2018, we uploaded a video for beginners called "How to Start a YouTube Channel from Zero." We didn't expect it to go viral, but that video quickly gained traction and has continued to get massive views. Today, it has over four million views and gets tens of thousands of views per month.[27]

You never know which video might be the one that blows up and opens your door to success. We were stacking the deck the whole time, and it paid off. While you can't control which video will be the one that does it for you, commitment to consistency creates the best chance to make it happen.

We interviewed Jerry from the tech channel *Barnacules Nerdgasm*, a YouTuber with over 800,000 subscribers. He told us, "Don't get discouraged if things happen slowly. It took me four years to get my first 10,000 subscribers, but it only took me two years to get the next 700,000."

CONSISTENCY BEST PRACTICES

How can you stay consistent?

---

27   Video Influencers, "How to Start and Grow Your YouTube Channel from Zero—7 Tips," YouTube video, 13:38, https://youtu.be/hwONmhK_pYQ.

We are full-time YouTubers. We post a ton of content on our channel, but we know how busy life can get. You've got family demands. You might have a full-time job, or you might be trying to build a business and want to use YouTube to market that business.

Just like you, we deal with several demands in our lives, so we've had to become efficient and strategic in creating content for our channel. Our strategy is composed of two essential things:

1. Scheduling in advance
2. Producing in batches

Prior planning prevents poor performance. Or, to put it another way, if you fail to plan, you plan to fail. Planning saves you a ton of energy, so we schedule filming days in advance. With batch producing, we set everything up—lighting, cameras, sound, stage—and film multiple videos in one session. We'll even change our shirts throughout the shoot to create the illusion of days passing.

Batch producing has been the essential element for creating a lot of content and being consistent in a minimal amount of time. *Video Influencers* runs a weekly interview show, which means we need to shoot and edit fifty-two videos a year. To make that more manageable, we do a few things. Sometimes, we go on mini tours, where we visit an area that has a few different people we'd like to talk to, and then we batch produce those interviews. Other times, we attend industry-related events and shoot ten to twenty interviews over a matter of days, giving us ten to twenty weeks of content.

If you have a full-time job, a family to take care of, or you go to school, then keeping it simple is better than nothing at all. When we're going through a busy time in our lives, we prefer to create simple, valuable videos that don't require a lot of extra production. We utilize graphics and videos to spice them up. We also love to go live. If you have the knowledge or expertise to talk about your channel's niche off the cuff, going live is an easy way to get content out there without the need for heavy editing.

Too many creators get bogged down in production, and they get overwhelmed with the amount of footage they have or the scope of their idea. Experimenting with different content formats allows you to stay more consistent on a week-to-week basis, whether that's going live for fifteen to thirty minutes and sharing some tips, shooting a short Q&A just to engage with your audience, or making a quick talking head video.

Scale back the complexity. That doesn't mean your content will suffer. It simply means you're being as realistic as possible about how much time you have, how many resources you have, and what it takes to post consistent content on a regular basis.

Almost every YouTuber we know, ourselves included, started off with talking head videos, low production values, and few resources. Even the channels that now create big, expensive videos didn't start off that way, so don't stress about it. Just start creating consistent content.

When Benji first started vlogging with his wife on their channel *It's Judy's Life*, they only had a cheap seventy-five-dollar point-and-shoot consumer-level camera. For years, they used that same camera, even when it literally fell apart at the screws. In 2015, they finally upgraded to a Canon point-and-shoot camera that cost around $750, but it's still nowhere near the high-end production of other successful channels.

In fact, all of their 3,400 vlogs in the last ten plus years were shot on low-to-high-end consumer-level cameras. The key to their one billion video views came not from professional equipment but from consistency, getting better daily, and Judy's gradual mastery of video editing through sheer repetition.

HOW OFTEN?

How consistent do you need to be? How often should you upload to YouTube?

Those are extremely common questions. The simplest answer is, "As often as you can." It depends, of course, on how busy your life is, and how challenging things are for you right now. If you can only manage one video a month, that's better than nothing, so long as you're consistent about it. Ideally, we recommend a minimum of at least once a week.

Too many beginners go hardcore, post tons of content up front, and then forget about YouTube. A study by Matt Gielen, who wrote an article about cracking the YouTube algorithm, reveals that YouTube prefers creators who post two to three videos per week.[28]

It's better to upload one video a week for fifty-two weeks and stay consistent throughout the whole year than to upload fifty-two videos in the first month and only upload sporadically afterward. You learn so much more about content creation that way, and your channel benefits from the long-term consistency. Plus, you can avoid burnout that way, because you're pacing yourself. Remember, it's

---

28   Matt Gielen, "Reverse Engineering the YouTube Algorithm: Part II," Tubefilter, February 16, 2017, https://www.tubefilter.com/2017/02/16/youtube-algorithm-reverse-engineering-part-ii/.

the consistent creators who get rewarded by both the audience and the platform.

If you have the bandwidth, the infrastructure, the passion, and the hustle, then don't feel limited to only posting once a week. Posting more than once a week will grow your influence faster.

At the end of the day, consistency is something you must have to succeed on YouTube. Consistent hard work leads to success, and from success comes greatness.

OUR SHOOT DAY CHECKLIST

- Block time on your calendar for the shoot. What gets scheduled gets done.

- Research your video ideas ahead of time. We've all heard the saying, "If you fail to plan, you plan to fail." The best creators on YouTube always do research before they press record. See the chapter on ranking for tips on how to do this.

- Outline the content of your videos. We don't read from a tele-prompter or script for our videos, but we like to work off simple outlines. We use Google Docs to create a bulleted list of things we want to make sure we include.

- Prepare your gear. Before your shoot day, make sure to charge your camera batteries. Lay out any gear you're going to use so there are no surprises when it's time to record.

- Select a location. A location that is well lit with minimal background noise is ideal when shooting videos.

- Prepare your wardrobe. We shoot multiple videos at once but release them over successive weeks, so we like to prepare simple shirt changes to indicate a passing of time and to create variety in our videos.

- Be purposeful with your morning routine. Go into your shoot day well-rested, focused, and confident.

- Shoot your videos. All of your preparation has led to this point. Hit the record button and own it.

- Shoot any B-roll. B-roll includes extra footage, clips, and transi-tion scenes that could support the main content you've recorded. Remember, if you begin editing and find out you need some footage, it will be very frustrating, so ask yourself while you're shooting, "Are there any other video clips I should get before I finish this session?"

- Shoot thumbnails. The thumbnail is one of the most important parts of a YouTube video, and trying to find a clear frame out of your video footage can be difficult. Getting a good thumbnail is as simple as turning on your camera's timer and getting an intentional photo of yourself.

- For more in-depth tips about shooting good video, check out the following video from *Think Media*: TubeSecretsBook.com/Checklist.

PART TWO

• • •

TACTICS

By having the courage to step out, clarifying your message, setting up your home base with your channel, uploading quality content, nurturing and building your community, beginning to monetize, and staying consistent, you lay a solid foundation for success on YouTube.

Next, we'll reveal some of the tricks, techniques, and ninja tactics to get you more views, more subscribers, and a bigger income. You've probably already started coming up with great content ideas, but we'll help you make the most of every opportunity. So, turn the page, and let's dive in.

CHAPTER 8

· · ·

THE PERFECT VIDEO RECIPE

Hey, Benji here. You know, I've been cooking for as long as I can remember. Initially it was purely self-serving—so I could eat home-cooked meals—but as I got older, the joy of watching others savor my cooking has become my primary motivation.

One of my favorite recipes to cook (and one that many have enjoyed) is lasagna. I've cooked lasagna hundreds of times, so I know the recipe by heart. It takes hours of careful preparation. The meat sauce has to simmer on low heat for a very long time, and I use a parmesan bechamel sauce between the layers. Trust me, it's delicious.

However, like any cook, occasionally I don't get the recipe just right. It happens to the best of us. One evening, I prepared lasagna for my family. I cooked it the same way as I always do, using all of the same ingredients. I prepped everything, stacked it up, threw it in the oven, and set the timer for an hour. Then I waited.

When I finally pulled the lasagna out of the oven and tasted it, something was slightly off. It didn't have its normal grandeur. The sauce was dry, and the cheese had burned a bit on the corners. Regardless of that fact, I served it to my family, and they still enjoyed it. It wasn't as good as I wanted it to be, but I learned from the experience, and I knew I'd get it right the next time.

Cooking is that way. A lot of things can go wrong. One incorrect ingredient can change the flavor. Leaving it on the heat just a few seconds too long can overcook it. One step out of place can screw up the whole recipe. And it's not just about the food itself. The presentation, ambience, and environment can also affect the end result. Serve great food with a bad attitude and people will enjoy it less.

Even when things go wrong, the final dish can still come out more than edible, but it could be so much better!

YouTube videos are the same way. Your goal is to create a final product that will satisfy a viewer's craving for top-notch content. You may not get all of the elements just right, especially early on, but if you do enough, you can still provide value for your audience. Keep their attention, meet their needs or expectations, and the end result (in terms of views and engagement) will be better than most videos that get uploaded to YouTube.

With cooking, if you spend time in the kitchen every day working on the same recipe, you will get better at it. Practice makes progress, and progress over time leads to the type of food that keeps people coming back for more. Eventually, you get so good that you can truly "wow" your family every time.

Similarly, with YouTube, you gather the ingredients, craft the video, and then present it to viewers with the goal of wowing them and making them want more.

By the way, to see an example of both my lasagna and the perfect video recipe, check out the following video: TubeSecretsBook.com/Lasagna.

THE METRICS THAT MATTER MOST

How can you hook the attention of viewers in the opening few seconds of your video and keep them watching until the end? It's like that first amazing bite of a good meal. The unfolding flavors make you want to keep eating until you've finished every bite. In fact, one of YouTube's stated priorities is "viewer satisfaction," so the goals of YouTube search and discovery are (1) to help viewers find videos to watch and (2) to maximize long-term viewer engagement.

YouTube viewers are always on the hunt for great content that will satisfy their hunger for entertainment, knowledge, or education, so you need the perfect recipe to really draw them in and keep their interest. In this chapter, we're going to show you what that perfect recipe looks like, but first, let's discuss the four primary ways that the YouTube algorithm (and content critics) will judge your videos. To chase our metaphor, it's a little bit like a chef trying to impress food critics (in other words, it can be quite tricky).

There are quite a few metrics contained in the analytics section of your YouTube channel, but if you want to impress the algorithm, the metrics that matters *most* are:

1. Clickthrough Rate (CTR)
2. Average View Duration (AVD)
3. Average Percentage Viewed (APV)
4. Average Views Per Viewer (AVPV)

You can see each of these metrics for every individual video on your YouTube channel, or you can see them averaged across all of your channel as a whole. Why are they so important? Because these four metrics most clearly illustrate the ideal viewer journey, showing how a video can go viral on the platform.

For a detailed walkthrough on where to find these metrics inside of YouTube Studio, check out the following link: TubeSecretsBook.com/Analytics. For now, here's an overview to get you started.

CLICKTHROUGH RATE (CTR)

A restaurant might have the most amazing food in the world, but if the name of the restaurant is unappealing or the pictures of the food online look really bad, a lot of people will avoid it. Similarly, you can make the most amazing video in the world, but if the topic, title, or thumbnail doesn't pique anyone's interest, then very few are going to click on it. Therefore, the perfect video recipe starts with an enticing presentation that grabs viewer interest.

In simplest terms, clickthrough rate is the number of clicks a video gets divided by the number of thumbnail impressions (i.e., how many times the video thumbnail is seen on YouTube). For example, if your thumbnail is seen a thousand times on YouTube, and a hundred people click on it, then you have a clickthrough rate of 10 percent. The reason this is so important is because YouTube is more likely to keep showing your video to new potential viewers if your clickthrough rate is high. A weak topic, title, or thumbnail usually contributes to a lower CTR, which can kill your video's chances of success.

> **Bottom line:** Your topic, title, and thumbnail must generate enough viewer interest to make them click on the video! If people don't click on your videos, YouTube isn't going to recommend them.

AVERAGE VIEW DURATION (AVD)

Once you've overcome the first challenge—getting a viewer to click on your video—the next challenge is getting them to keep watching. This is why "video views" can be a misleading metric. A bunch of people might click on your video because of a striking thumbnail but then only watch an average of three seconds before bouncing off to some other video. It's like a diner in a restaurant ordering a dish because it looks interesting, taking one bite of it, then throwing the rest of it in the garbage.

"It looked amazing, but it tasted horrible!"

Average view duration is the total watch time of your video divided by the total number of video plays (including replays). Essentially, it's measuring your ability to engage viewers and keep their attention. If your video fails to keep viewers, they'll bounce away fast, leaving you with a low AVD. This matters because YouTube's number one priority these days is to keep viewers on the platform as long as possible.

If your video keeps people watching for five minutes, that's great. For ten or twenty minutes? Even better. AVD is *not* dependent on the length of your video. All that matters is the total number of minutes watched. Your mission, should you choose to accept it, is to get your average view duration as high as possible by keeping viewers watching your video for as long as possible.

> **Bottom line:** Minutes matter most! Get your AVD as high as possible by keeping viewers watching your video for as long as possible.

AVERAGE PERCENTAGE VIEWED (APV)

Average percentage viewed measures *how much* of a video viewers watch. For example, if you post a ten-minute video, and a viewer watches it for five minutes, then your APV would be 50 percent.

How does average percentage viewed differ from average view duration? We're glad you asked. Here's an example that should clarify. Sean uploaded a tutorial on his *Think Media* channel that is forty-four minutes long. It has gotten over 1.2 million views, and the video continues to be recommended by the YouTube algorithm, getting roughly a hundred views per hour.

Why does YouTube keep recommending it? Because the average view duration is eight minutes and fifty-seven seconds, which is twice the average view duration of most videos on YouTube. That's great! At the same time, the tutorial is very long, and people rarely make it through all 44 minutes. Consequently, even though the AVD is high, the average *percentage* viewed is only 20.4 percent. That's not so great.

Nevertheless, people are watching, on average, just under nine minutes of the video. Getting hundreds of people every hour to watch nine minutes of video is still pretty good. Remember, YouTube's ultimate goal is to get people to spend as much time as possible on their platform. If you can get hundreds of people every hour to watch nine minutes of video, the algorithm will continue to promote your video to new people.

> **Bottom line:** APV measures how much of a video's total length people are watching. While minutes matter most, it's important to get people to stick with you until the end of a video by keeping them interested.

AVERAGE VIEWS PER VIEWER

Average views per viewer (AVPV) is a little harder to find on YouTube Studio because it's contained in something called "advanced mode," which gives even more insights into how your channel and videos are performing.

Let's use our food analogy again. If you run a local burger

joint, getting discovered on Yelp is good, getting the customer into the restaurant is better, and convincing them to order multiple dishes and have a great experience is better still! However, *none of that* is the ultimate goal.

The ultimate goal of your restaurant is to create loyal customers who will frequent the place for years to come. Similarly, when it comes to your YouTube channel, it's great to get new viewers to watch one video, but it's even better to get them to binge multiple videos in a row. However, the ultimate achievement is to create super fans who will watch all of your new content for years to come.

You do this by getting a click (CTR), holding the viewer's attention for as many minutes as possible (AVD, APV), and capturing their interest enough to get them to watch multiple videos in a row on your channel (AVPV). If your average view per viewer is five, it means that on average people who watch your channel will watch five videos in a row.

Let's suppose each of those videos is five minutes long. That means the average viewer spent twenty-five minutes on your YouTube channel engaging with your content. As far as the algorithm goes, that's what winning looks like on YouTube.

Now, we're not saying that getting a high clickthrough rate

(CTR), keeping viewer attention (AVD, APV), and getting them to watch multiple videos in a row on your channel (AVPV) is easy. However, if you understand these four metrics then you will have a distinct advantage in getting YouTube to recommend your content, because now you know exactly what to work toward.

> **Bottom line:** AVPV measures how many videos viewers watch on your channel in a given period of time. YouTube loves when you can keep people engaged with your content by getting them to watch more videos on your channel.
>
> For a detailed breakdown on where to find these metrics in your YouTube Studio, along with additional insights on triggering more video views, check out TubeSecretsBook.com/Analytics.

THE INGREDIENTS OF A WINNING VIDEO ON YOUTUBE

To make an amazing meal, you first have to acquire the right ingredients and bring them all together. Once you have the right ingredients, you also want to bring together some spices to kick up the flavor. The same goes for your YouTube videos. If you want to create winning videos, you need to bring together the right ingredients and add the right spices.

There are four primary ingredients you need to create a winning YouTube video:

1. Big Idea
2. Hook
3. Core Content
4. Quick Transition to Another Video

Let's look at each of them.

THE BIG IDEA

You start creating your amazing YouTube video long before you press record on the camera. Just like Hollywood screenwriters trying to create the next blockbuster film, you first have to come up with a big idea for your video. The big idea is communicated to potential viewers through your (1) topic, (2) title, and (3) video thumbnail.

In Hollywood, the big idea, or *topic*, of a movie is generally expressed as a one-sentence pitch called a "logline." Here are some examples of loglines from famous films:

- *Elf:* A Christmas elf goes to New York City.
- *The Matrix:* A computer hacker learns from mysterious rebels about the true nature of his reality and his role in the war against its controllers.
- *The Lion King:* Lion cub and future king, Simba, searches for his identity. His eagerness to please others and his penchant for testing boundaries sometimes get him into trouble.

- *The Godfather:* The aging patriarch of an organized crime dynasty transfers control of his clandestine empire to his reluctant son.

In Hollywood, the logline is critically important. If it doesn't grab the attention of studio executives, they're not going to fund it and the movie won't get made. As YouTube creators, we can learn from this process. If you can't describe the big idea for your video in a strong, compelling logline, then your idea might not be interesting enough to capture viewer interest and make them click.

We're not suggesting that you have to create a logline for every YouTube video, or that every video must have some groundbreaking idea behind it. However, if you want to have any hope of getting thousands, even millions, of views, then the big idea for your video had better be strong.

Once you have a big idea, you need to create a powerful *title* that will hook viewer attention by creating curiosity and interest. You should also plan your *thumbnail* ahead of time, even if you have little more than just a basic concept or a screenshot of other thumbnails or images as inspiration.

Often, top YouTube creators will brainstorm multiple video ideas, design thumbnails to pair with those ideas, and then evaluate if they're worth creating. Only one out of five ideas might actually end up being created. This may sound like a waste of time, but it's a great way of coming up with your best ideas.

Remember, just having all of the ingredients doesn't guarantee an amazing dining experience. You also need to cook them at the right temperature, plate them well, and serve them with a smile to someone who likes that kind of food. Similarly, coming up with a big idea is about getting clarity on your audience and convincing them to click with a compelling topic, title, and thumbnail.

THE HOOK

Once you've convinced a viewer to click on your video, you need to give them a powerful opening that will let them know they made the right decision. This is called "the hook," and it should give viewers a glimpse of what's to come so they will want to watch until the end.

Has something like this ever happened to you? Scrolling through your favorite streaming service, you come across a reality TV show with a title, description, and thumbnail that seemed interesting to you. So, you click on the show and start watching. In the first few minutes, they provide a few short, dramatic scenes that give you a tantalizing glimpse of what is to come in the episode. That's the hook! They are trying to convince you to keep watching to the end by providing you with a look ahead.

"See this dramatic fight between characters? It's coming up later, so keep watching the show!"

Actually, Benji does exactly the same thing in the lasagna video we talked about earlier in the chapter. During the first few seconds of the video, he tells viewers what to expect while showing them tantalizing visuals of the cooking process and even a glimpse of the final dish. In essence, Benji is telling viewers upfront, "Here is the amazing dish you'll be able to make if you'll watch this video to the end."

It's a promise to viewers: "Stick with me, and I'll make it worth your time."

On many YouTube videos, the hook might only be ten to twenty seconds long, a simple statement of what is to come, but it's possible to create something much longer. In fact, a hook can be almost any length as long as it does its job.

The hook is such an important part of any YouTube video that we could probably write a whole book about it. Actually, our friend Brendan Kane did just that. It's called *Hook Point: How to Stand Out in a 3-Second World*. Feel free to check it out.

However, to get started, we recommend spending a little

extra time planning the hook for your video. What can you say that will let viewers know that the information or entertainment they're going to get from watching your video is worth their time? Make a promise to viewers so they won't regret having clicked on your video. Think about some clips you can use to tease the action that is coming up later.

One of the biggest mistakes we see creators make is limiting their hooks to a long-winded speech about themselves, often with an intro "bumper" that contains music and an animated logo. These simply take up too much time early on. Get to the point, share your big idea, and give viewers a glimpse of what is to come. That's all you need to do.

If you want a long-winded speech about yourself, save it for later in the video. Keep it out of the hook! Remember, you want to keep viewers watching as long as possible, so if you lose people in the first few seconds with a weak hook, it will kill viewer retention and your video won't perform well.

CORE CONTENT

Your core content is the meat of your video. Now, you might wonder how long the ideal YouTube video should be. The answer is there's not a magic number. Tightly edited five-minute videos can perform well on YouTube, and so can hour-long educational videos. If you keep delivering value to an audience that is interested in your big idea, you have a chance to perform well.

Still, if you're just starting out, shorter is probably better. A new viewer who doesn't know you yet is more likely to risk five minutes of their time checking out one of your videos before they'll spend forty-five minutes with you. We recommend testing videos of different lengths to find your sweet spot. As a best practice, remember that fast-paced content that delivers value will always perform best.

When it comes to your content, our friend Chalene Johnson says, "Be brief, be bright, make it fun, and then be done."

ADDITIONAL INGREDIENTS THAT WILL SPICE UP YOUR VIDEOS

Anything you can do to make your videos more interesting will help you keep viewers longer and win new viewers faster. Think of them like the spices you add to a dish to make it taste even better. You don't need all of them, but adding a few here and there will kick up your video a notch.

- **Visuals and Video Clips:** Adding extra footage to your videos, called "B-Roll," is one of the best ways to keep viewer attention as long as possible.

- **Video Editing:** While editing your videos isn't required, using things like jump cuts, transitions, and graphics will almost always make your videos more interesting.

- **Camera Presence:** Unless you create a faceless YouTube channel, you have to work on perfecting your camera presence. Commit to getting just 1 percent better on camera with every upload. You can do this by studying great communicators and content creators, watching the most viewed TED talks, and practicing, practicing, practicing. When you do this, you will be amazed by your progress over time.

- **Preparation:** Just because YouTube is free for anyone to upload, it doesn't mean you should upload disorganized stream-of-consciousness videos. A better approach comes from asking, "Who exactly am I making this video for? What value do I want the person to get out of this video?" Take a few minutes to organize your content, thoughts, and ideas, and you'll go a long way toward making your videos significantly stronger.

- **Get to the Point:** Cut out the boring, non-essential parts of your video. Trim the fat! Make it half as long and twice as strong. The YouTube algorithm will reward you.

- **Humor:** One of the best ways to keep a viewer's attention, especially if you're presenting a lot of information, is to use humor. Don't force this if it doesn't come naturally, but consider lightening the mood by sharing your personality along with a joke or two. As Mary Poppins said, "A spoonful of sugar helps the medicine go down."

- **Music:** With music, you can set the mood, create energy, and keep viewers watching longer. A word of warning: make sure to use copyright-free music, or your video may get flagged or lose monetization. The YouTube Music Library is a free resource that provides 100 percent copyright-free music for creators. There are also paid resources like Epidemic Sound.

- **Sound Effects:** Adding appropriate or amusing sound effects makes your video more entertaining. By combining sound effects with music, you have the best chance of keeping viewer attention longer and earning new views faster than a Tesla in "ludicrous mode."

QUICK TRANSITION TO ANOTHER VIDEO

If you're successful with your big idea, the hook, and the core content of your video, then viewers should be hungry for more. Your final goal is to quickly transition *out* of the core content and invite viewers to watch another video on your channel.

The video you recommend should complement the video they've just watched. Make it a "part two," a next step, or a video on a related topic. Remember, your goal is to increase the average view per viewer (AVPV), so ideally, the viewer will continue to travel further down the rabbit hole of your channel's content. Point the way, so they know where to find more and more videos that might interest them.

The best way to do this is to use YouTube "end cards," which are a feature in YouTube Studio that allows you to select a specific video in your library that will show up on screen during the last twenty seconds of your video. The viewer can click on the image of the video, and YouTube will take them directly to it.

Power Tip: Don't let viewers know you're ending the video. Since the first edition of this book, social media has gotten more crowded and noisier than ever. There are now over sixty *billion* messages posted on digital platforms every single day! The average person is exposed to somewhere between four thousand and ten thousand ads every twenty-four hours. Inundated with choices, consumers must make decisions within milliseconds. A common mistake we see among creators is letting viewers know a video is over as soon as the core content is done. A related mistake is waiting forever to ask viewers to subscribe or extending the video outro. As Brendan Kane explains in his book *Hook Point*, "It takes three seconds to make or break your business."[29] Most viewers will stop watching your video as soon as they realize the core content is done, so your only chance to keep them on your channel is to quickly transition them to other videos.

By combining these four ingredients (big idea, hook, core content, quick transition) with the eight additional spices, mixing them well, and cooking them to perfection, you will create a high-quality video that boosts the metrics that matter most to the YouTube algorithm. When you do that, your video will perform much better, and it might even go viral!

If you're just getting started, all of this might feel a little overwhelming. Don't sweat it. The occasional mess-up in the kitchen is normal. It happens even to the best cooks. We've given you the perfect video recipe so you have a

---

29   "It Takes 3 Seconds to Make or Break Your Business," Hook Point, accessed February 12, 2022, https://hookpoint.com/about/.

template that will give you much better results, but don't be afraid to mess up. Don't assume that you have to use all of these ingredients and spices from the get-go.

Everyone who has ever learned to cook has burned a few meals, forgotten some ingredients along the way, and created a few dishes that didn't taste good. What makes someone a world-class chef is sticking with it, learning, practicing, and improving over time. It's exactly the same on YouTube. Your first videos will be your worst videos.

As we said earlier, make it your goal to get 1 percent better with every upload. Small tweaks will lead to giant peaks, so don't be hard on yourself. Don't compare the first chapter of your YouTube journey to the twenty-fifth chapter of someone else's. Just commit to doing the work and "staying in the kitchen."

Now that you've posted a video to YouTube, it's time to increase your reach even further using social media, so turn the page, and let's see how you can use social media platforms to boost engagement on your YouTube channel.

CHAPTER 9

. . .

SOCIAL MEDIA: THE GOOD, THE BAD, AND THE UGLY

"Don't use social media to impress people; use it to impact people."

—DAVE WILLIS

What's your favorite beverage? We're big fans of coffee, which is no doubt influenced by the fact that we both grew up in the Pacific Northwest, home of Starbucks. Since its founding, Starbucks has grown into a global coffee empire with over 349,000 employees and a net value of over $30 billion.[30] However, the company went through a period where they almost lost everything because they lost their focus.

---

30 Sean Dennison, "Starbucks Net Worth: How Much Is Starbucks Worth and Is It Worth Investing?" GO Banking Rates, accessed November 4, 2021, https://www.gobankingrates.com/money/business/how-much-is-starbucks-worth/.

By 2003, Starbucks' meteoric rise had peaked. Because of overconfidence, and perhaps a bit of arrogance, company leaders had begun to think they could do anything. "We're bigger than coffee," they said. And so, Starbucks created its own recording company. By 2006, they had launched their first movie, partnered with the William Morris Agency to scout for music, books, and films, and even opened their own entertainment office in Los Angeles.

Marketing experts wrote gushing articles about this creative expansion, praising the company's ingenuity, but Starbucks paid a price. They poured so much energy and effort into their new business avenues that they struggled to maintain focus on what they did best: making a great cup of coffee.

By 2008, that lack of focus had caught up to them. Their most loyal consumers began to complain about the "cracks" in their service and quality, and many switched from Starbucks to local coffee houses that focused solely on making coffee. As a result, Starbucks was forced to cut 18,000 jobs and close 977 stores, and same-store sales dropped 7 percent across the board. The stock price fell by $7.83, to a low of $39.63. The company was in big trouble.[31]

---

31 Graham Robertson, "Case Study: The Starbucks Come Back Story: Losing Their Focus, Only to Regain It!!!" LinkedIn, September 17, 2014, https://www.linkedin.com/pulse/20140917165734-13996180-case-study-the-starbucks-come-back-story-losing-their-focus-only-to-regain-it/.

Ultimately, it served as a wake-up call for leaders to refocus on what Starbucks did best. They eliminated most of their "extracurricular activities" and doubled down on coffee. By 2014, sales were up 58 percent compared to 2009, the stock price soared, and they've continued to grow ever since.

SOCIAL MEDIA MIGHT BE YOUR BIGGEST ENEMY

In the first edition of *YouTube Secrets*, this chapter talked about how important—how essential—social media is to your success on YouTube. However, we've learned quite a bit over the last few years, studied the YouTube algorithm extensively, and grown our online businesses a lot. As a result, our mindset on social media has radically changed.

So, what's our opinion now? If you're a YouTube creator trying to balance school, work, and other responsibilities with creating and posting videos consistently on your channel, *social media might be your biggest enemy*.

Why? Because social media is a distraction that robs you of time and energy that you should be using *on* YouTube to achieve your goals faster. We've watched countless creators wasting hours and hours trying to post regularly on every social media platform and getting burned out, and for all of their hard work, they only get lackluster results.

When it comes to social media, you need to ask yourself, "Is this the best use of my time?" The answer is almost certainly a resounding *no*.

WHAT'S THE BEST WAY TO GROW ON YOUTUBE?

As it turns out, the best way to grow your YouTube channel is with YouTube itself. A single video that breaks out and ranks in YouTube search or gets recommended by the YouTube algorithm will have vastly greater impact than trying to build an audience on every social media platform and move them to YouTube.

Spending time and effort building engagement on multiple social media platforms to feed your YouTube channel is a little like Starbucks trying to produce movies and music instead of focusing on coffee. It dilutes your efforts and will slow or stop your overall growth.

According to countless case studies that we've seen, trying to send traffic from Facebook, Instagram, TikTok, or LinkedIn to YouTube is almost never effective. For example, the mindset of the typical Instagram user is to keep scrolling their feed, liking videos, watching short reels, and direct messaging friends. From our own research and personal experience, less than 5 percent of Instagram users, possibly as few as 1 percent, will actually go to your bio to click on a YouTube link or "swipe up" on your story. Even worse, because of that Instagram mindset, even if they do click over to your YouTube video, they're unlikely to watch more than a few seconds, which hurts your average view duration (AVD).

On the other hand, if someone searches for something specific on Google or YouTube and comes across your video, they are more likely to watch until the end. Why? Because their intent from the start is to find the information you're providing. If someone purposely logs into YouTube on their computer, phone, or smart TV, their intent is to spend time on the YouTube platform. They *want* to check out the latest uploads from their favorite channels and videos recommended by the algorithm.

That doesn't mean you should never post on Facebook, Instagram, or Twitter to let your followers know about your latest YouTube video, but it's not an effective way to trigger significant growth for your YouTube channel. Just keep that in mind. More than that, it can cloud your focus.

For that reason, we strongly recommend spending most of your time and energy on making the best possible videos following our perfect video recipe. Even after you start gaining momentum on YouTube, avoid the temptation to spread yourself too thin too soon by expanding your content creation effort to other social media platforms.

Starbucks was hitting a peak of their success when they were seduced into losing focus. Don't fall into the same trap.

WHEN AND HOW SHOULD I USE SOCIAL MEDIA?

Does that mean you should avoid using social media altogether? Not necessarily. It depends on your business model, the season of your YouTube journey, and the resources you have available. In the following sections, we'll discuss the best ways to use social media as you progress through the three "seasons" that YouTube creators go through: the side-hustle season, the solopreneur season, and the scale season.

SEASON ONE: THE SIDE HUSTLE

How do you know when you're in the side-hustle season? When you're not yet earning a full-time income from YouTube and your online business. During this season, the majority of your time is spent at a part-time or full-time job. You might be in school, committed to volunteer work, or raising a family. Whatever the case, time is probably scarce, so you must be wise about how you spend it.

Now, if you already have a massive following on TikTok or Instagram, it makes sense to shout out your new YouTube channel on your social media platforms to send as much of your audience as possible to your channel. However, most people in the side-hustle season start at zero on every platform.

It's important to focus most of your energy on creating YouTube content, learning and leveling up your YouTube skills, and leveraging the platform's new features. We will discuss these new features in Chapter 15, but for now, make the decision to concentrate on your YouTube channel. It is, by far, the best way to grow.

A good question to ask yourself during this season is, "What's the shortest path to making money, so I can devote more time and attention to growing my YouTube business?" Use the strategies in this book to get views, so you can turn those views into cash, as we discussed in Chapter 6. If you want to do YouTube full-time, this must be your main focus. The work is hard, and time is short, so aggressively avoid distractions!

Nevertheless, during this season of your YouTube journey, we recommend creating a presence on the most relevant social media platforms for your audience and niche. Don't spend time creating original content on those platforms just yet. Instead, use them to connect to other people. In particular, you can use them to reach out to other creators for collaboration, or you can contact brands to try and initiate sponsorships.

It's also useful to secure your name and social media handles on multiple platforms so you can use them later. You will be able to build on them later once your income and resources have grown.

During the side-hustle season, remember this advice from Michael Jordan: "Focus like a laser, not a flashlight."

That's exactly what Sean did when building *Think Media*. He largely ignored social media, using Instagram and Facebook only to post personal life updates about his family and connect with loved ones. His sole focus was on making YouTube videos that ranked in search and then connecting them to smart monetization strategies, like affiliate marketing. This focus played an essential role in getting him to the next season of his YouTube journey.

SEASON TWO: SOLOPRENEUR

Congratulations! At this stage, you've quit your job because you can now cover all of your expenses with the money you're earning online. Now, you find yourself on a treadmill, trying to do it all and hoping the money will keep coming in.

Entering the solopreneur season is a significant milestone that deserves to be celebrated, but you must stay vigilant to protect your focus—especially when it comes to social media. You need to ask yourself again, "What is the best use of my time?"

To that end, you should develop some clearly defined goals and ambitions at this point and define exactly how much time you can devote to your YouTube business. Maybe you're able to spend forty to sixty hours a week on YouTube, or you might limit yourself to twenty hours and spend the rest of the time with family, with friends, or working on other projects and hobbies.

Here's our best advice: double down on what's working on your YouTube channel. Try to increase the number of high-quality videos you post each week. You might start expanding content creation to other platforms at this stage of your journey, but be careful not to lose focus.

Benji interviewed Ben Schmanke from *AuthenTech* on our *Video Influencers* Live Show. Ben has been a full-time creator and "one-man band" for a few years, growing his channel to more than four hundred thousand subscribers and creating a six-figure business while maintaining a great work-life balance with his wife and two kids.

According to Ben, "When you are building a YouTube business, it's very easy to get distracted."[32] Therefore,

---

[32] Video Influencers, "The YouTube Lifestyle: Tips and Tricks from a Full-Time YouTube Creator w/ Ben Schmanke," YouTube video, 27:50, https://youtu.be/RYvILZNGl4I.

his first priority each week is to post at least one video, possibly two. After he has accomplished his main goal, he spends some time on what he calls "supplementary channels." TikTok, Instagram, and Twitter are his favorites because he considers them a funnel leading back to his overall brand as a tech expert and educator.

Ben has made the most impact on TikTok, where he's grown his following to more than one hundred thousand people, getting over 1.4 million likes on his videos. He has also created another revenue stream, earning a small additional income from the TikTok Creator Fund and getting a sponsorship deal with Hewlett Packard.

One benefit of experimenting on other platforms, according to Ben, is that you learn a lot in the process. Indeed, Ben likes to experiment with short-form ideas, creating powerful hooks that are only a couple of seconds long, but he calls YouTube the "king platform," because that's where he earns most of the income that supports his family. He may get millions of views on TikTok, but his financial return there is a fraction of his YouTube income.

Ben knows where his priorities lie, so he stays focused while also experimenting, expanding, and diversifying on other social media platforms. During his interview with Benji, he expressed that he's "having a ton of fun messing around on TikTok and seeing what hits."

That's the power of staying focused while expanding during the solopreneur season. Don't neglect your core source of revenue—YouTube—but you've earned the right, and created enough margin, to spend as much time on social media as you want to, especially if you enjoy it.

SEASON THREE: THE SCALE SEASON

According to leadership expert John Maxwell, "One is too small a number to achieve greatness." Maxwell believes that teamwork is the heart of great achievement.

We will discuss building a team in Chapter 13, but the key to the scale season is that you are no longer a "do-it-all" solopreneur. Now, you've built a team to help you accomplish your mission, and you can use some of those team members to keep up with your other social media platforms.

Keep in mind, the biggest mistake you can make with social media is trying to imitate what someone else is doing when you lack their resources. For example, best-selling author, business leader, and YouTube celebrity Gary Vaynerchuk says, "If you are not producing a hundred pieces of content...every single day you are leaving the greatest opportunity in the world on the table."[33]

---

33   Team Garyvee, "18 Moments to Explain Why You Should Post 100x Per Day," Gary Vaynerchuk, 2019, https://www.garyvaynerchuk.com/create-content-100-pieces-per-day/.

A statement like that can make you spit out your coffee!

"A hundred pieces of content a day?" you might think. "I would die if I tried to sustain that!"

Are we contradicting Gary Vaynerchuk? We just told you to largely ignore social media, but Gary says you need to massively up your social media game. So, who's right?

All of us, actually. You see, Gary has 3.5 million subscribers on YouTube, but he also has over one thousand employees working in his businesses, including a dedicated team of more than thirty people who focus exclusively on building his personal brand. One way they do this is by taking his keynote speeches and turning them into social media content. A single speech can be turned into sixty-four different pieces of content that get distributed across Facebook, Twitter, TikTok, LinkedIn, Pinterest, YouTube, YouTube Shorts, Instagram, Snapchat, Discord, Medium. com, email, text, and other platforms.

By the way, if you'd like to learn the system that Gary's team uses for creating content, check out Gary's free SlideShare at TubeSecretsBook.com/64PostsPerDay.

Ultimately, out of the hundreds of successful YouTube creators we've interviewed, the vast majority have a team working behind the scenes. Very few have thirty full-time employees like Gary, but many have family members helping them part time, or a virtual assistant, or even a full-time contractor from Upwork.com who does administrative work and social media.

There are also services that will turn your YouTube videos into microcontent pieces that you can spread across social media. Ben Azadi of *Keto Kamp* uses Repurpose House, which will create clips from your videos in square, vertical, and landscape formats with your custom branding for less than $500 per month. You still have to submit the timestamps in the video where you want the video clip cut, as well as write a catchy headline so social media users will stop scrolling. Ben also uses a virtual assistant who handles posting the clips on his social media platforms.

So, how long can you expect to be in each season of your YouTube journey? It depends. Sean was in the side-hustle season from 2010 to 2015, finally going full-time at the end of 2015. However, he immediately realized that he needed help, so he started building his team. Even with a few people assisting at *Think Media*, social media did not become a priority, as he doubled down on posting videos to YouTube and creating his own products. His goal was to produce "more money for the mission," so he could impact more people and recruit additional team members before expanding into new territories.

If you're just starting out, trying to imitate the volume of content that Sean posts on social media would be a huge mistake. *Think Media* now has a twenty-person team. It's no longer a one-man side hustle like it was in 2010.

Stay focused! Be ruthless about eliminating distractions, time-wasters, and low-value tasks that don't get you closer to your goals. By staying focused, you will make money faster, free up more time, and enable yourself to build a support system to help you achieve your personal vision for the channel. Remember, the key to the third stage, scale season, is to put a team and systems in place that will enable you to create consistent quality content on social media sustainably.

THE POWER OF SOCIAL MEDIA TO HELP YOU SCALE

Benji's story is a great example of how planting seeds early on can lead to fruitful opportunities down the road. In the beginning, he focused most of his time on his YouTube channel and business. Once he had momentum, he began signing up for rising platforms like Facebook, Instagram, and Snapchat, posting as often as he could, if not daily, to stay connected and grow a following over time.

His following on these platforms didn't make a major difference for his YouTube videos, but it built depth with his audience and grew a deeper connection. Years later, after acquiring hundreds of thousands of followers, and developing a core followership, his social media has led him to some awesome opportunities. In addition to his six-figure annual income from brand deals, he has been able to use his clout to connect with other influencers for collaboration and maximize his business ventures.

His relationship with his audience is priceless. If he hadn't started his social media years ago, he wouldn't be nearly as large of an influencer, and his fans wouldn't be as deeply connected to him.

THE SECRET KEY TO EVERY SOCIAL MEDIA PLATFORM

If you want to grow on a particular social media platform, you have to learn and master the best practices for that platform. Moving an audience from one platform to another is rarely effective unless you have a massive following. Even then, it's difficult, but you must understand the platform to make it work.

For example, the best way to grow on Instagram is to post amazing content on your Instagram feed, optimize your profile, post Reels, utilize Instagram Live, and upload longer-form videos using Instagram Video.

The best way to grow on TikTok is to create great, consistent content that gets recommended by the TikTok algorithm.

The best way to grow on LinkedIn is to optimize your profile and post meaningful text, photos, videos, articles, and live streams, and experiment with new features like LinkedIn Stories.

Don't forget the importance of responding to comments, writing comments on other people's posts, and connecting with people in direct messages (DMs).

Personally, we love social media, despite our strong warning at the beginning of this chapter. It works if you invest enough time and energy into it. However, time and energy are scarce resources, so pick your battles wisely when you're starting out. Over time, you can build an army to help you win more battles on new fronts.

CREATING YOUR SOCIAL MEDIA GAME PLAN

Cal Newport, author of *Digital Minimalism*, encourages content creators to choose a focused life in the noisy world. As he puts it, "We are over-hyping the benefits of social media and way underplaying the negatives and the costs."[34]

---

34   Mark Brouwer, "While Everyone is Distracted by Social Media, Successful People Double Down on These Key Skills," Medium, July 18, 2019, https://medium.com/@markbrouwer/while-everyone-is-distracted-by-social-media-successful-people-double-down-on-these-key-skills-4536feccdf33.

So, if you're still struggling to get clarity on how best to use social media to grow your YouTube channel and online business, we recommend asking yourself the following questions:

- What season are you in, and what is the best use of your time right now?
- Where is most of your growth on YouTube coming from?
- Would it be better to do more of what's already working rather than starting something new?
- Who is your target audience, and what social media platform are they most active on?
- If YouTube is your primary focus, what would be the best additional platform to start using to reach your target demographic?
- Are you already maximizing the potential inside of the YouTube platform by using the Community tab, YouTube Stories, YouTube Live, and YouTube Shorts? (We'll discuss these in more detail in Chapter 15.)
- Which social media platforms do you use for family, friends, and fun? Which social media platforms will you use for growing your online business?
- What should you *stop* doing so you can focus on your greatest strengths and highest impact?

In the end, social media is neither good, bad, nor ugly. It's simply another tool you can use, and its value comes down to how you use it. We have no doubt that it will continue to be a major player in the next decade, and it will remain a powerful tool for building your YouTube channel, your online business, and ultimately, your legacy if you don't lose focus.

Focus is power. Learn the lesson of Starbucks. Keep your highest impact activities at the core of your daily routine.

In the next chapter, we'll show you how to create a video that will keep getting views and making money for you on YouTube for years to come, so turn the page and let's see how you can make YouTube work for you while you sleep.

CHAPTER 10

. . .

DISCOVERABILITY: ATTRACT YOUR IDEAL AUDIENCE ON AUTOPILOT

"The best place to hide a dead body is on page two of Google."

—ANONYMOUS

Businesses and brands understand the importance of getting their website and content to show up on the first page of search results. Becoming the answer to their target audience's inquiries can make or break a business. Getting to the first page means the difference between moderate and massive success.

Google remains the number one search engine for just about everything, but very few people know what the second largest search engine is. Can you guess? Is it Bing?

Is it Yahoo? No, actually, it's YouTube. People forget that YouTube is essentially a search engine. This search capability presents a massive opportunity for you to get discovered. YouTube's search volume is larger than that of Bing, Yahoo, AOL, and Ask.com *combined*.[35]

WHAT IS DISCOVERABILITY?

When someone searches for something relevant to your channel on YouTube's search bar, you want your video to show up in the first few results. If one of your videos shows up high on the list of recommended videos, you can get views and subscribers whether you post new content or not.

For example, on Benji's cooking channel, he posted a video about cooking stovetop popcorn. If you go to the YouTube search bar and type in "stovetop popcorn recipe," his video will show up at one of the top spots in the search results. Try it for yourself and see. This is cool, of course, but let's dive a few layers deeper. At the time of writing this second edition, his video was getting thirty-nine views per hour. When you add that up, that's 936 views per day, which adds up to 340,000 views per year.

---

35 Adam Wagner, "Are You Maximizing the Use of Video in Your Content Marketing Strategy?" *Forbes*, May 15, 2017, https://www.forbes.com/sites/forbesagencycouncil/2017/05/15/are-you-maximizing-the-use-of-video-in-your-content-marketing-strategy.

One huge thing to note here is that this video is over seven years old and has gotten over two million views. Benji spent time creating that video once upon a time, but it continues to work for him, getting discovered by as many as one thousand new people per day. That is the power of climbing to the top of the search results, so don't neglect strategically optimizing your videos for search if you want to build your influence.

Sean posted a video in 2015 titled, "What Is Amazon Prime and Is It Worth It?" The video continues to be viewed daily, but it has also become a major source of passive income because Amazon pays a bounty of three dollars every time someone signs up for an Amazon Prime trial. When you combine the power of YouTube search with smart monetization strategies, your income can grow very quickly.

Would it benefit you to get your brand's YouTube channel seen by one thousand new people a day? We're not talking about paid advertising. We're not talking about putting gas in your car and driving through your neighborhood, going door-to-door to generate awareness for a product or a service. We're not talking about hiring a PR company to promote you. What we're talking about is tapping into this free platform called YouTube and leveraging the massive discoverability factor of getting your content to show up in search results. This isn't something you should only do occasionally. Climbing the search rankings needs to be part of your ongoing growth strategy.

If you go to YouTube and type in "cheap cameras for You-Tube," you'll discover one of Sean's videos has gotten over 2.8 million views over the last few years. How can you do the same for your videos? Once Sean discovered the power of YouTube Search, he committed to creating a library of videos that would rank in search. It started slow—one video at a time. Not every video ranked, but some did. And some videos that were created ten years ago continue to get views! Today, his channel *Think Media* gets 6,000 views every sixty minutes—that's 250,000 views every two days. It's like a freight train of continuous views from YouTube. The momentum is crazy!

ENHANCING DISCOVERABILITY

Let's take a look at a few ways you can enhance your own videos so they rank higher in search results. What we're talking about is called Video SEO (search engine optimization), which refers to the process of optimizing your videos to make them generate interest not only with your current subscribers but also with YouTube's search engine.

When you utilize SEO, you make it easier for the search engine to know if that video is relevant to viewers' searches. Get this right, and your videos will start climbing the ranks.

The most important aspects of Video SEO on YouTube are your title, thumbnail, and content that keeps the viewer watching, as we shared in the chapter on the perfect video recipe. But the secret is actually the video topic: creating videos that people are actually searching for.

Discovery starts with figuring out what people search for. Once you discover a strong video topic, it will dictate the rest of the video creation process. To enhance your video discoverability, ask yourself, "What are the top ten to twenty questions that my target audience is searching for on YouTube?"

One practical way of doing this is by using the YouTube search bar itself. If you've been using YouTube for long, you may have noticed that when you start typing something into the YouTube search bar, it provides a list of pop-up predictions underneath your search.

What you might not realize is that those predictions come from what people around the world are searching for. They represent the most searched terms related to whatever you're typing in. For instance, if you type "how to cook bacon" in the search bar, the predictions that pop up will represent different recipes that people like to search for.

To take advantage of this feature, figure out what your

target audience is searching for by looking at the search bar predictions and create content that addresses those topics, questions, or inquiries in a relevant way.

Don't try to cover too many topics in one video. Rather than trying to make a video about ten different breakfast recipes, make ten different videos, each one focused on a specific recipe. Instead of a video covering all kinds of breakfast cooking topics, make one video on cooking bacon, another on making fresh-squeezed orange juice, and another on cooking the perfect eggs. Often, content creators go too broad. You'll get far better results by creating narrowly focused videos to address specific questions that your audience is asking.

To continue with our bacon example, create a title based on the exact phrase YouTube predicted and include variations of that same phrase in your description, as well as the tags. For example, Benji titled his video, "The Easiest Way to Cook Bacon." In the description, he included variations of that same phrase, and the tags included things like "how to cook bacon," "bacon in the oven," and "bacon tutorial."

If you're in the fitness niche, you could create a workout video with a title like, "How to Get a Fit Body for Men at Home." To stretch your content further, break that video into multiple, smaller videos, each focusing on more specific topics like "Men's Bicep Workout," "Men's Leg Workout for Mass," and "Men's Shoulder Workout Routine." By breaking that one long video into three smaller, more specific videos, you create three different ways for people to discover your content.

If you go to the YouTube search bar and type in, "How to stay motivated," followed by a space, YouTube will provide numerous nuanced predictions like "How to stay motivated to lose weight," "How to stay motivated to work out," "How to stay motivated on YouTube," "How to stay motivated to study," and "How to stay motivated in tough times." Notice that each of those examples provides dramatically different video ideas. While one might apply to fitness, another applies to the *Video Influencers* niche: how to stay motivated on YouTube. Use this method to discover some strategic video ideas that will help get your content discovered on YouTube searches.

You can do this in any niche, because people ask questions about practically every topic. Your goal is to discover what those searchable video ideas are and create quality, strategic content around those terms.

Creating search-based content is one of the best ways to start getting views when you're new, and it can lead to millions of views over time. However, search traffic on YouTube is only responsible for 10 percent of the traffic on

YouTube.[36] By the way, if you're new to the term "traffic," it essentially means "views" or "visitors." We use the terms interchangeably throughout this book.

Another aspect of discoverability on YouTube that you can tap into is "suggested" or "related" videos. The biggest source of traffic on YouTube is suggested videos. More than 70 percent of what people watch is determined by the recommendation algorithm.[37] Suggested videos appear on the YouTube home page, in a sidebar on desktop computers, below the video on mobile, or at the end of the video a person is currently watching.

When you take some time to do topic research, follow the perfect video recipe, and avoid cutting corners on optimizing your video description and metadata, you will give your videos the best chance of getting traffic from both search *and* suggested. Entertainment channels typically get most of their views from being recommended by the YouTube algorithm, while education channels often get most of their views from search. Your goal should be to tap into both.

Sean's channel *Think Media* falls into the education cat-

36   Roberto Blake, "YouTube SEO: YouTube Suggested Videos Algorithm Deep Dive," May 5, 2020, https://robertoblake.com/how-to-get-youtube-to-suggest-your-videos/.

37   "YouTube by the Numbers: Stats, Demographics & Fun Facts," Omnicore, January 3, 2021, https://www.omnicoreagency.com/youtube-statistics/.

egory, so 40 percent of the more than 3.5 million views the channel gets monthly come from YouTube search and 26 percent come from suggested videos. That equates to over 2.3 million views per month! Benji and his wife's vlog channel, which falls into the entertainment category, gets an average of five million views. Seventy-five percent of those views come from YouTube suggested videos, and only 5 percent come from search.

It's another reason why YouTube is so amazing. New people can discover your content by directly searching for specific topics *or* from YouTube observing their viewing behavior and recommending your videos to them.

OPTIMIZE CONTENT BEFORE YOU CREATE IT

To incorporate discoverability into your overall video strategy, always research before you press record. The goal is to determine if there is widespread interest in the video topic you're considering creating and use that interest to inform your video title. A huge mistake we see people make is recording videos and trying to optimize them afterward. We believe you should reverse that order. Strategically plan the big idea, title, and thumbnail of your video before you start filming. That way, you'll be able to create the most relevant content possible for the exact thing people are searching for. As we mentioned, you can use the YouTube search bar to quickly come up with video ideas. Simply enter the terms and look at the predicted responses.

For even greater insights, including discovering how many people per month are interested in specific topics, we like to use tools such as KeywordsEverywhere.com, Wordstream.com, and vidIQ.com. If we had to pick just one, our favorite tool for keyword research and topic research is vidIQ.com. For a quick tutorial on how to use it, check out TubeSecretsBook.com/vidIQ.

The keys to making this work are (1) getting crystal clear on the intent of viewers who are searching for your content, (2) titling your videos so they speak directly to those viewers, and (3) making sure the content in the video delivers on the promise you make in the title. For example, let's say you're in the lifestyle and beauty niche, and you create an advanced makeup tutorial but title it "easiest makeup" because you found that title in your research. That wouldn't be strategic, because your content is not in alignment with what the viewer is looking for. That example might seem obvious, but it's those types of subtle nuances that will make or break this strategy. Google and YouTube want to serve their users the best possible content for their inquiries, so the more aligned your content becomes with those answers, the higher your content will rank.

This focus on Video SEO needs to happen from day one, before you have a single subscriber. In fact, SEO should be a priority from the moment you begin planning your channel. If you build it into the foundation of your channel, you will generate more traffic long-term. A well-designed video with a focus on SEO will continue to get recommended long after you've forgotten about it.

Practice makes progress. As you begin to incorporate Video SEO into your content, you'll get better and better. *However, the best Video SEO in the world won't do any good if your content isn't good.* Valuable and engaging content that has been strategically positioned and optimized is a combo that can't be beat.

We've shared the basics on ranking videos in this chapter, but YouTube continues to make updates that require new strategies and new approaches. If you're interested in learning the exact details of the best new tools and software for finding money-making video ideas, ranking them, and monetizing them in multiple ways, check out Sean's free one-hour web class at TubeSecretsBook.com/FreeClass.

Once you start to climb in the rankings, garnering more views and getting discovered, you open the door to collaboration with other successful YouTubers. That's what we'll look at next.

CHAPTER 11

• • •

COLLABORATION: GROW YOUR AUDIENCE EXPONENTIALLY

"Competition makes us faster; collaboration makes us better."

—MAHFUZ ALI SHUVRA

In the early '90s, West Coast hip-hop grew in popularity and authority on the music scene. In 1992, the classic single "Nuthin' but a 'G' Thang" reached number two on the Billboard Hot 100 and number one on the Hot R&B/Hip-Hop Songs chart. The song was a duet by American rappers Dr. Dre and Snoop Dogg from Dre's debut solo album, *The Chronic*. It elevated Snoop Dogg to a wider audience and gained him tremendous exposure. As impressive as he was when guesting on Dre's *The Chronic*, few guessed he'd go on to global fame, millions in record sales, and a career in movies and TV.

Interestingly, Snoop Dogg has sole songwriting credit on "Nuthin' but a 'G' Thang." Dre provided the larger platform and audience, while Snoop brought his talent for writing chart-topping songs. The collaboration proved to be a huge win for both artists.

Collaborations can be powerful in art, music, film, business, and YouTube. Smart influencers don't sit back and hope for results. They act intentionally in cultivating powerful relationships and pursuing collaborations.

There's no better way to get people to take interest in you than someone they trust and love referring you to them. Because of this, we believe collaborating is one of the fastest ways to grow your viewership, second only to viral video.

COLLABORATING WITH OTHER CREATORS

There are three main benefits of collaboration.

- *It exposes you to a new audience.* The influencers you collaborate with often have already established an audience within a specific demographic or tribe of viewers.
- *It spreads out the work.* When you collaborate, sometimes you cut the work of video creation in half and multiply the success.

- *It helps you learn.* Pharrell Williams, musician and entrepreneur, said, "Collaborate with people that you can learn from."

Additionally, collaboration expands your network and leads to friendships and business relationships.

THE QUALITIES TO LOOK FOR IN A COLLABORATOR

What qualities should you look for in a good collaborator? Make sure they have some level of alignment with your niche. We discourage people from working with other YouTubers simply because they're famous. If their audience doesn't align with yours, collaboration won't drive the right exposure to your content.

For instance, if you have a tech channel focused on photography, cameras, and lighting, you don't want to collaborate with someone who has a cooking channel. It could be fun, but it might not be the best way to get in front of your target audience or generate the right kind of exposure.

However, just because someone has a different type of content doesn't mean their audience isn't relevant. For example, let's say there's a YouTube influencer who specifically focuses on NFL news and information, and your channel shares game day recipes for football fans.

Though these channels offer different kinds of content, the audience aligns through a mutual interest in football. Consider the general interest and lifestyle of the audience of a potential collaboration channel. Even if your channel focus differs from that of a potential collaborator, their audience might still find it relevant and exciting.

When considering a potential collaboration, get familiar with their content and values. Watch their past videos, check out their social media feeds, and evaluate their audience. Look at their YouTube channel, and if you can't find any collaborations, it might indicate that they don't heavily engage in it. That doesn't mean you shouldn't reach out, but it's something to bear in mind. On the other hand, if you discover they've done numerous collaborations, the chances of getting them to work with you are much higher.

WHY WOULD PEOPLE COLLABORATE WITH A NEWBIE?

You're just starting out. You don't have a large audience yet. Why would anybody want to collaborate with you?

First of all, you can add value to their channel by providing more content. Even if you're relatively unknown, creators love when you contribute to their channel. Adding value isn't just about the content itself. You can also save them time. Established creators often struggle to find enough time to create all of the content they want to create. By helping them out, you give them a great reason to collaborate, even if your audience is small. Offer to help with setting up the shoot or editing the video.

Second, you may have special skills, knowledge, experience, or authority that will allow you to do things with their content that they can't do on their own. For example, on his channel, Benji talks about cooking and shopping for food; however, it's impossible for him to know everything. Oftentimes, he collaborates with other creators who have way more knowledge than he does about specific topics.

When talking about the difference between organic and conventional foods, he collaborated with RawBrahs, brothers who live a natural food lifestyle, (even though they had a relatively smaller audience) because they are far more knowledgeable on the topic of organic food. Thanks to their expertise, that content not only provided great value for Benji's viewers, but also allowed RawBrahs to do much of the heavy lifting in terms of the content, not to mention the cross-promotion to both audiences.

Third, you might provide fresh ideas for another YouTuber. Any creator who has been around a long time knows that coming up with creative ideas can be challenging. A new YouTuber brings fresh ideas for their channel, which is a huge relief to an established channel in danger of becoming stagnant.

Fourth, you can provide technical support. Just because someone is a full-time YouTuber doesn't mean they know how to use all the tools of the trade. Many famous You-Tubers use simple point-and-shoot cameras. If you're a photographer or videographer, if you have access to high-quality gear, you present an opportunity for them to have a more highly produced piece of content.

Collaboration is how we, the Video Influencers, connected. When we met, Sean discovered that Benji and his wife were established YouTubers, whereas Sean was focused more on video production and behind-the-scenes work. It led to a great collaboration. Sean brought a unique set of skills, and, as mentioned in Chapter 6, we worked on a project together called *The Wedding Series* that ended up being a win-win for us. Benji worked in front of the camera and Sean served as director and videographer behind the camera, a team dynamic that laid the foundation for Video Influencers.

Don't ever hesitate to reach out, even if you're just starting. We forget most people like to help others, and it never hurts to ask. Asking doesn't guarantee you're going to get a yes, but not asking guarantees you never will.

FINDING AND REACHING OUT TO COLLABORATORS

Create a spreadsheet of people you would love to collaborate with. We use Google Sheets to keep up with our ever-growing list of people we want to collaborate with and interview. This puts them all in one place, along with their social media accounts, any contact info we can find, and notes so we can strategically reach out to them on a regular basis.

People are busy these days, and their inboxes and social media feeds are crowded. We recommend checking with people once a quarter or twice a year. Cycle through your list.

Power Tip: The more people you reach out to for collaboration, the higher the chances of getting a yes.

When searching for other creators on YouTube, the best chance for success typically comes from channels the same size as yours. Of course, everybody wants to collaborate with bigger, more successful channels, but those people get far more requests. Someone with an audience the same size as yours is more likely to respond positively. Having said that, remember that audience size isn't as important as shared audience interests and similar content chemistry.

The best way to collaborate with a larger or more successful YouTuber is to approach them with an interview request. With an interview, you don't position yourself as a peer. Instead, you position yourself as someone who's going to help them share their information, wisdom, advice, and insight with a wider audience. It requires a low level of commitment from them. Tools like Zoom and StreamYard make recording or streaming an interview fairly simple. That allows you to interview people from anywhere in the world and share that interview on your YouTube channel.

The interview method has worked great for us. Not only have we interviewed channels of similar size, but we've managed to get creators with much larger audiences as well. When we only had ten thousand subscribers on our *Video Influencers* channel, we were able to get content creators with multiple millions of subscribers to agree to interviews.

One of the ways we got the yes was by focusing on adding as much value as possible. For example, if a creator was writing a book, we shared information about the book with our audience. Our goal was to provide a high-quality interview, promote their content and projects, and hustle as hard as we could to share the interview, so we could honor the time they took to do the interview with us. Another great way to reach potential collaborators is through events. In the YouTube space, live events like VidCon, Playlist Live, CVX Live, VidSummit, Video Marketing World, Grow with Video Live, and ClamourCon continue to grow in popularity. They present great opportunities to meet people you would love to collaborate with. If you're intentional and strategic, you can set up collaborations ahead of time and record them during these events.

Also, by attending events, you can network and plant the seeds for future collaborations. Get involved in local events as well, even if they aren't directly related to your niche, because they provide opportunities to meet new people you might want to collaborate with later.

We always look for local social media, video production, small business, and entrepreneurship events, and through them, we have created many important relationships. Most of our collaborations happen during these events, and often, we set them up on the day of the event. If people are willing to spend the time, money, and effort to attend a special event, there's a high chance they're also open to an invitation to shoot a collaboration video or be interviewed on the spot.

Earlier, we talked about the power of batch-producing content by shooting multiple videos at a time. Events are great for this. At an event in Palm Springs called ClamourCon, we shot twenty interviews in two days. It was a lot of work, and we didn't have much brainpower left by the end of the second day. However, we left the convention with twenty weeks' worth of videos created from one batch. So, while attending an event might cost a lot of time and money, the payoff can exceed what you spend.

There are a few ways to reach out to people you'd like to collaborate with. The first one is Twitter. We love using Twitter because it's an appropriate platform to talk to anybody. Think about how you might creatively tweet other influencers to set up possible collabs.

Another great option is direct messaging. In particular, using Instagram DMs has become quite effective. Bear in mind, when you message somebody who doesn't follow you, your message might end up in their spam folder. Don't let that stop you. Many people check their spam folders periodically, so they might find your message. If you message a hundred people, a handful could say yes. That makes the effort worthwhile.

Important note: Don't start your message or DM with a solicitation. We recommend starting by expressing gratitude for their content or using some organic engagement to begin the conversation. If the influencer you reach out to has a ton of people messaging them, a spam message probably won't get read.

Most YouTube channels have an email address specifically for business inquiries on their "About" page. Also, look for Facebook groups or other online communities where influencers in your niche gather. These are great places to discover people to build relationships with.

Whichever strategy you use, never adopt an aggressive approach. Consider how you can reach out creatively, how you can get noticed without being forceful, weird, or generic. When people reach out to collaborate with us, one of the quickest ways to get ignored is if it's obvious they're simply copying and pasting the same message to multiple people. We love it when it's apparent people have watched our content, have knowledge about our body of work, and reach out in thoughtful and personal ways. That increases the chances of us collaborating with them.

> **Power Tip:** One of the biggest mistakes we see people make when reaching out for collaborations is only focusing on themselves. Don't do this. Authentically engage with their content first, learn about what's important to them, then position the "ask" based on how you can add value to the other person, not what's in it for you.

People have been collaborating on YouTube since the beginning, and many have experienced massive success as a result. Never be afraid to approach a popular YouTuber and ask—you never know who might say yes.

One of Benji's favorite collaborations started with someone canceling a collaboration. He flew to New York City to interview a well-known influencer. The morning of the interview, that person's schedule changed, so they had to cancel the meeting. He'd traveled a long way, so the situation was frustrating, as you can imagine.

However, it was what he did the day before that made it all worthwhile. When he arrived in the city, he emailed another creator, knowing the person also lived in New York City. Remember, it never hurts to ask. He was surprised to learn that the other creator was more than willing to meet with him. His name? Casey Neistat, winner of GQ's New Media Star in 2016, Best First-Person Series Online from the Streamy Awards in 2016, and a YouTuber with over twelve million subscribers.

He invited Benji to his studio, where he conducted the interview. He also shouted out the interview on his channel and linked to it in front of his subscribers. A day that started off as a disappointment turned out to be a huge opportunity.

Collaborations are super powerful. Start cultivating those opportunities right now, but don't get discouraged if they don't happen right away. These things take time. However, in the next chapter, we'll share a strategy that you can do right now to start growing your YouTube channel faster than ever before.

. . .

CHAPTER 12

TRENDS AND TENTPOLES: CONSPIRE WITH THE CULTURE

"You need to go where the opportunity will be next, not where it is."

—JEREMY GUTSCHE

We live in an age of viral memes, video challenges, and internet hypertrends—of the Harlem Shake, Planking, and the Mannequin Challenge. One popular internet trend was called "The Ice Bucket Challenge," sometimes called the "ALS Ice Bucket Challenge." This activity involved dumping a bucket of ice water over a person's head to promote awareness for the disease Amyotrophic Lateral Sclerosis (ALS). It went viral on social media during July and August of 2014. It took the internet by storm and helped raise $115 million for research, helping scientists discover a new gene tied to ALS.

While many internet trends may seem wacky and random, participation can be a very smart strategy for content creators. On YouTube, timing is everything. Holidays, seasons, viral videos, popular songs, current movies, and events all create opportunities for relevant content. Incorporate them to ride the momentum and exposure these trends produce.

WHAT'S A TREND?

A trend is a viral moment happening in internet culture. Once a trend sparks interest, it spreads like wildfire throughout the internet. We already mentioned a few relatively recent examples, like the Harlem Shake, Planking, and the Mannequin Challenge. If you're not familiar with them, take a moment to search for examples on YouTube. Other trends include popular products, such as fidget spinners and hoverboards.

Smart influencers jump on trends by incorporating them into their content or doing product reviews and monetizing them through affiliate marketing. When fidget spinners gained popularity with young people, smart YouTubers found all sorts of creative ways to use these simple little toys to gain greater exposure.

Gossip about current events can also create trends. One of the most famous and longest-standing YouTubers,

Philip DeFranco, has capitalized on this since the beginning of his YouTube channel. Philip DeFranco's channel covers news and topic-of-the-day content, and he does it very well. He's great at researching to find the most viral headlines or gossip topics of the moment. Then he talks about the topics and provides his own personal insights. Because he connects to trending topics, many people find his videos without being subscribed to the channel. That one simple strategy has grown his audience to more than six million subscribers and garnered him over two billion views.

Emily D. Baker, a former LA District Attorney, regularly live streams on YouTube, breaking down the details of legal cases involving famous YouTube creators and celebrities. The public's interest in the juicy details of these cases, along with her expertise and insights into the legal documents, helped her YouTube channel grow to over one hundred thousand subscribers in just six months. Her growing community is affectionately called "Law Nerds," and her rapid success has led to a highly profitable at-home business.

You can also jump on current events that tie into your industry. If you remember, back in 2017, Samsung had huge issues with their Galaxy Note 7 phones blowing up. Literally blowing up. They were so prone to exploding that they were banned from airplanes. While this created horrible news for Samsung, smart influencers in the technology niche jumped on this in the form of commentary and comedy, riding the wave of its popularity and shareability. YouTuber JerryRigEverything posted a video of a phone actually exploding and got over 7.2 million views on that one video alone.

HOW TO CAPITALIZE ON A TREND

When it came to the ALS Ice Bucket Challenge, content creators from all backgrounds, industries, topics, and professions jumped on it. Not only did it raise awareness for a great cause, but many people found it interesting and entertaining to watch people have freezing cold water poured over their heads. From entrepreneurs to celebrities, musicians, and stay-at-home moms, all kinds of people participated.

Even if your industry is highly professional, you should still consider jumping on these kinds of cultural trends. Never forget that people do business with people. If you let your hair down and show your staff having a little fun and getting a bit crazy, that makes for great content that could be shared on your social media platforms or on your YouTube channel.

Even though we advised you to focus on your niche, the great thing about a trend like The Ice Bucket Challenge is that its trendiness makes it applicable to just about any channel. Even if the challenge is off topic, it gives you a way to make a human connection and have fun with the broader culture. Your loyal viewers will be forgiving.

Another way you can capitalize on trends is by covering popular songs or pop culture moments. For example, family vloggers Sam and Nia have grown their channel to over two million subscribers. What many people don't know is one of the early reasons their channel grew was because of a viral video they posted of singing "Love Is an Open Door" from Disney's *Frozen* while driving in their family minivan. That video received over twenty-three million views while they were in the early days of building their influence. Consider how you could incorporate pop culture, music, and movies into your content to achieve a similar result.

You can also capitalize on trends by weaving popular influencers into your content. For example, on Sean's tech channel, *Think Media*, he created a video about Casey Neistat's video gear. Casey had posted a video that gave a generic overview of his gear, but it didn't go into detail. Sean saw the video and realized that other people would be interested in a complete breakdown, so he made that video. He provided a specific, detailed description of the gear Casey used and posted it the day after Casey posted his own video. Sean's video went on to get almost four hundred thousand views because it helped people find the video gear details they wanted. It also provided exposure for Sean's channel, which is focused on camera gear and video accessories.

Always look for ways to integrate trends into your regular content. Anytime a trend hits popular culture, ask yourself, "How can I capitalize on this trend while staying on brand?" For example, if you have a recipe channel, what are some trending recipes you could integrate into your content? One trend that gained popularity in the entrepreneur community was "bulletproof coffee," which entailed adding butter and MCT oil to your daily coffee, for its brain-enhancing effects. As the coffee recipe began to grow in popularity, smart YouTube creators took advantage of the trend and many of the videos they created received twenty thousand to over two million views!

Look at what's trending on social media in your niche and incorporate it. Be intentional and strategic about how you weave trends, viral content, and cultural events into your content. Don't forget that speed matters when it comes to trends. As soon as you see the opportunity, act fast so you can get your content out before the wave crashes.

WHAT IS A TENTPOLE?

We've talked about trends and their power to help you grow your influence on YouTube, but you should also pay close attention to tentpoles. What is a tentpole?

A tentpole is a way of capitalizing on recurring events and holidays throughout the year. For example, let's look at Halloween. People get interested in Halloween months before it occurs. That is the beginning of the tentpole. When interest peaks, that's the center of the tent. That's the time when the most searches are done. This typically occurs right around the actual holiday. After the day passes, interest falls dramatically and quickly. In the case of Halloween, interest starts in September, builds up throughout October, peaks on the thirty-first, then drops off almost immediately the very next day.

Holidays comprise the most obvious tentpole events: New Year's, Valentine's Day, St. Patrick's Day, Halloween, Thanksgiving, Christmas, and sometimes-overlooked holidays like Mother's Day, Father's Day, and consumer events like Black Friday in the United States and Boxing Day in countries like the United Kingdom, Canada, Australia, and New Zealand. Every single one of these holidays provides an opportunity to create and schedule strategic, relevant content on your channel.

Outside of holidays, major cultural events can become tentpoles. Examples include the Super Bowl, the Academy Awards, and gaming events like E3. Basically, any major cultural event creates an opportunity for YouTubers to create relevant content as interest rises. Try to keep up with relevant cultural events, like elections, the next big *Star Wars* movie, or anything else generating interest. The seasons are tentpoles, so if you have a lifestyle or a fashion channel, consider creating video content around seasonal outfit ideas.

Outside of holidays and cultural events, popular industry-specific events can also become tentpoles. The Consumer Electronic Show (CES) is one of the largest electronics expos in the world. If you have a tech channel, it's a perfect niche event you can capitalize on. Even if you can't attend the event, you can still create relevant content and commentary in the days leading up to it. Take advantage of the event hashtag on Twitter, Instagram, and other social media platforms. Join the conversation before, during, and after the event. This maximizes awareness and exposure for your channel.

TAKING ADVANTAGE OF A TENTPOLE

The most important aspect of an effective tentpole strategy is to jump on a topic early in the tentpole journey. So, if you're creating content around Halloween, don't wait for interest to peak. That's too late. Start posting relevant content when people begin searching for Halloween costumes, Halloween recipes, Halloween *anything*. That happens a few weeks to a couple months before the actual holiday. When you post relevant content early, you beat other creators to the punch, which means you have less competition for views and more time to gain momentum when searches are highest, better positioning yourself for ranking.

A great tool for tentpole strategizing is Google Trends (trends.google.com). This tool shows, with precise specificity, when the interest and search traffic begins, accelerates, peaks, and diminishes for holidays, cultural events, and trends of any kind. Additionally, consider combining other strategies we've shared in this chapter. For example, if you want to collaborate with another YouTuber, schedule it around a tentpole to enhance and strengthen the value of the trend.

Last, remember, fortune favors the fast. Plan your tentpole strategy far in advance and have a strategic content calendar to jump on trends and tentpoles as early as possible. Sometimes life gets busy, so you will miss a few events now and then. Still, we encourage you to do whatever you can to make the most of the big tentpole events, even if that means canceling plans, staying up late, or pushing yourself to get content done.

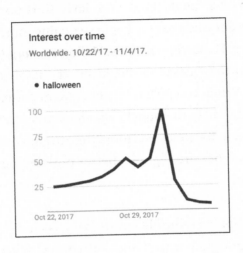

EXERCISE: TREND AND TENTPOLE LIST

Write down a few creative ideas for tentpoles and trends in your niche. On Sean's tech channel, that means including things like Cyber Monday and Black Friday. Knowing those events happen in late November, Sean starts planning and preparing the content in October, if not earlier. Benji, as a food enthusiast, considers different recipes for Thanksgiving and Christmas early in the fall to take advantage of early searches.

By planning early, you can release content at the beginning of each tentpole for maximum exposure and views.

If you're using YouTube for business, what industry events could you weave into your content? If you're in the lifestyle and beauty niche, consider creating videos about the looks and styles of trending celebrities. Strategically plan your videos as fashion fads change.

No matter what niche you're in, trends and tentpoles drive new awareness to your YouTube channel, but they certainly aren't the only way. In the next chapter, we will discuss a behind-the-scenes strategy for scaling and growing your influence and creating more content on YouTube through the power of teamwork.

CHAPTER 13

. . .

TEAM: SCALE YOUR VISION

"Talent wins games, but teamwork and intelligence win championships."

—MICHAEL JORDAN

Why do birds fly in a V formation? As each bird flaps its wings, it creates an uplift for the bird immediately following. By flying in a V formation, the whole flock adds at least 71 percent greater flying range than if each bird flew on its own. When you surround yourself with people who share a common direction and sense of community, you can get where you desire to go much easier, because you travel on the thrust, energy, and momentum of one another.

By now, you've realized that YouTube and social media take a lot of work. Though many people get started on YouTube individually, we recommend thinking about building a team from day one. In this chapter, we're going to share some thoughts, ideas, and tips on how to do that.

FINDING A TEAM WHEN YOU'RE STARTING OUT

We've never met a super successful influencer who didn't have a team, whether that means a personal assistant, a cameraman, a talent manager, or a full-on production studio. Your team is whoever supports you in building your YouTube channel, especially when you have other priorities that divide your time. Do you have a day job? Are you going to school? Do you have a family to take care of? Then you need to think about creating a team. Friends and family can absolutely be your teammates. Do you have a spouse who helps pay the bills or take care of the kids? That's your team.

One of the biggest mistakes creators make is to not communicate a compelling and unifying vision with those closest to them. Have you shared your vision for building your influence online with your family and friends? Have you asked and given practical ways in which they could support you? Initially, building a team is not about hiring people. It's about enlisting people already in your sphere of influence.

Unless you already possess the resources to hire a team, your first hires must be practical and low cost. What are the tasks the people in your life could help you accomplish? Additionally, consider ways to optimize and offload things from your schedule. For instance, maybe hiring a house cleaner or setting up a meal delivery service like Home Chef would save you a few hours a day, so you can work on your YouTube channel.

Benji served as his wife Judy's first team member, as her business manager and personal assistant. However, when the channel got more successful, they both found they were too busy to complete simple tasks around the home, so he began looking for help with basic chores.

His first hire was a kid in the neighborhood who wanted to make some extra money. Benji had mentored him in a program at the YMCA, and he knew the kid didn't have a lot of opportunity for work because of his age. He paid him ten bucks to mow the front and back yard. This was still early enough in Benji's YouTube career that saving time with something as simple as landscaping was a huge help. Ten years later, that same kid, all grown up, progressed to become a full-time production assistant for him.

Who in your immediate surroundings could help take over some daily tasks for you?

Today, Sean's YouTube channel, *Think Media*, and affiliated channels and businesses are run by a team of twenty people, but it didn't start that way. It started with Sean making videos by himself while his wife Sonja did the bookkeeping for their side hustle.

In the early days, when *Think Media* was just beginning to grow, Sean asked a friend from church if he would be interested in helping edit his videos. He had expressed interest before, so it was a perfect match in Sean's eyes. This turned into a summer internship. The friend worked in exchange for training and information. Not only was it a win-win situation, but it was a value exchange rather than a money exchange. Sean thought outside of the box. When it comes to enlisting support, you must be open to new, creative, and unique opportunities like this.

NEXT STEPS IN TEAM BUILDING

Once you're a bit further along, it's time to consider the next step in building your team. If you've accrued a little money, you can consider outsourcing services like graphic design or closed-captioning.

Closed-captioning, or subtitling, your videos makes them viewable to a wider audience around the world and ensures they rank in YouTube searches. YouTube has been making it easier to close-caption your own videos, but many creators prefer to use services like Rev.com to save time. As of this writing, Rev only costs $1.25 per minute for transcriptions and three to seven dollars per minute for foreign subtitles.

Need some graphic design updates for your YouTube thumbnails, cover images, or social media images? Fiverr. com has services as low as five dollars per job for all of your graphic design needs. You can even hire a virtual assistant on a site like Upwork.com. You don't have to hire someone for an insane amount of time. Hire help for just five hours a week, delegating tasks you aren't good at or don't enjoy.

Where in your life can you buy yourself more time to focus on what's most important? First, list the priorities for your channel, whether that's filming, editing, optimization, distribution, engagement, sustaining cash flow, branding, email, general inquiries, customer service, or managing a team.

Second, list the tasks that you tend to procrastinate in doing. Now, compare the two lists and note which tasks appear on both of them. Look at the tasks that are ranked the highest. That's where you need to start your outsourcing.

Consider how affordable outsourcing is. If your normal hourly rate in your professional life is twenty dollars an hour (and we'd argue your time is worth much more than that), and it takes you two hours to edit a video, then you could say it costs you forty dollars to edit a single video. If you hire an editor who will work for fifteen dollars an hour, assuming they can also edit the same video in two hours, then you've saved yourself five dollars an hour. Now you can spend those two hours focusing on your strengths and generating more income.

Most people, when they start making a little money, spend it on things and experiences. While that is great, if you are serious about scaling your business and brand on YouTube, we recommend investing your extra money by leveraging the skills of others to do more work than you could do on your own.

One of Sean's early hires was a person he met on Twitter who expressed interest in learning about video. However, they met at a time when he was unable to pay her any money. Fortunately, she didn't need a job. She only wanted to learn about online video and how to start earning a side income with YouTube. They entered into an agreement where she would receive a percentage based off the money earned from helping with Sean's YouTube channel. This was great because she was willing to embrace the risk of not getting paid, but if she did good work and performance increased, then she would get paid. The relationship started simple, but they were able to grow together because teamwork helps you grow faster, increase revenue, and ultimately experience more success. The risk paid off for her, and today, she is an executive at *Think Media* and one of the content creators on the channel.

To find help, reach out to people on social media. Make a Facebook post and let people know you're looking for someone interested in an internship. Find relevant networking events in your city using MeetUp.com. Consider looking for creative professionals in your area on LinkedIn. Get the word out among your friends and acquaintances. You never know what could happen. Don't limit yourself to conventional ways of thinking about team building. Our channel (and this book) is evidence that there are many people in the world who are interested in succeeding on YouTube. You'd be surprised how many are looking for experience and are willing to work for free for the opportunity to learn. You may be able to find some of those people in your own community. In fact, they may already be subscribed to your channel and following you.

OTHER SUPPORT SYSTEMS YOU SHOULD CULTIVATE

When we talk about teams, we're not just referring to the people who work directly to help you produce content. We also believe in having a winning circle of friends and mentors who help encourage you along the way.

Motivational speaker Jim Rohn famously said, "We are the average of the five people we spend the most time with."

After interviewing many Video Influencers, as well as associating with many successful entrepreneurs, we've noticed that they are all intentional about surrounding themselves with a world-class circle of geniuses. They want people around them who think big, challenge them, and give advice throughout the various stages of growth. You should do the same.

When it comes to surrounding yourself with mentors, there are three levels to consider. First, you have access to mentors through content. That involves reading books, watching videos, and listening to podcasts and other educational resources that inspire you, encourage you to think bigger, and give you the latest information for scaling your vision.

Second, you can attend conferences and industry events, surrounding yourself with like-minded people and expert speakers who will help you level up in every area. We make it a priority to attend multiple conferences in our industry every year. We don't do this simply to create content at those events, but also to meet people and learn from them while we're there.

Like the biblical proverb says, "As iron sharpens iron, so

one person sharpens another."[38] In other words, you need other leaders around you who can challenge and prepare you for the next level of success.

Third, you can invest in coaching. This might be as simple as a one-hour Skype call with an industry expert, or you can go much deeper. The bottom line is, you must be highly intentional about surrounding yourself with a support system for every level of your journey toward success.

Being a YouTuber and an entrepreneur can be lonely. Often, it feels like an emotional roller coaster. There will be times when you're on the top of the world, and other times when you don't want to get out of bed. Creating a circle of success around you is one of the keys for succeeding in every season.

Look at our example. We're both YouTubers. However, we bring different skills and experiences to the table. When we started our side project called Video Influencers, Benji was responsible for managing and operating the business, building the team, and bringing his vlogging experience and network into the partnership. Sean was responsible for creating the content, optimizing the videos, website and funnel building, graphic design, product creation, copywriting, and the online marketing strategy and execution. We built Video Influencers as a side project over the last

---

38   Proverbs 27:17.

six years, and it's become a success because we work as a team. Together, we bring different ideas and skillsets, so we stand out in a sea of other influencers. In the next chapter, we will dive deeper into how discovering your unique skills, personality, and perspective can help you achieve greater success on your journey to building an influence, income, and impact with online video.

CHAPTER 14

. . .

THINK DIFFERENTLY: CRUSH CONVENTIONALITY

"If you're doing what everyone else is doing, you're doing it wrong."

—CASEY NEISTAT

One of the fastest-growing channels in YouTube's history was that of Casey Neistat. In a short time, he grew to over twelve million subscribers and took the YouTube world by storm. He brought something new to an established genre, and thus, he not only grew fast, but he also won numerous awards.

Before Casey, people understood "daily vlogging" to be an established genre that included mostly casual videos of the content creator's life, often shot on simple point-and-shoot cameras with low production values. The strength of vlogging was believed to be the personality of the individual, not the production value of the content.

Casey brought a radically new approach to the genre. First, his camera setup was far beyond the point-and-shoot or smartphone quality that 99 percent of vloggers used. In fact, Casey's camera rig was outrageous. He also leveraged his exceptional video editing skills to create much higher production values. While most vloggers spend an hour or two editing their vlogs, Casey spends anywhere from four to eight hours (or more) per episode.

Furthermore, Casey's storytelling ability is unparalleled by most in modern media. Ultimately, he combined over a decade and a half of his life experiences, video production expertise, and a unique perspective on the world to create something that was new, different, and unique, and his channel grew in popularity very quickly as a result.

Nowadays, at most YouTube conferences, it's common to see vloggers walking around with the "Casey Neistat vlogging setup." What once looked outrageous is now the desired camera rig of many vloggers. He changed the genre.

Up to this point in the book, we've given you a framework for success on YouTube. We've given you specific tactics and strategies to help you grow, but we never want you to get the idea that there's only one set way to build your influence on YouTube. We hope we've given you guideposts, best practices, and a tool belt of resources that can get you big results, but ultimately, you need to carve your own path in any creative endeavor.

STAND OUT FROM THE CROWD

Often, what makes a channel unique comes from the personal experiences in a creator's life. What are the life experiences, personal or professional relationships, or areas of expertise you can use to make your YouTube channel different? A great example of this is Andru Edwards, a tech influencer who focuses on consumer electronics. He reviews products and shares tips, tricks, and insights on everything tech.

Of course, there are many tech influencers on YouTube, but Andru was also, at one time, a professional wrestler. As a wrestler, he always needed to have high energy, be entertaining, and be ready to perform at a moment's notice. When he first started his tech channel, he utilized these skills and charisma to add more entertainment value to his content.

In addition to that, his branding was unique. As a professional wrestler, being flashy and standing out contributes to a wrestler's brand, so when starting his tech channel,

Andru set himself apart with flashy clothes, bright colors, and a fashion swagger most in his niche did not have.

For your channel, you want to combine the best practices of successful YouTubers along with some unique qualities of your own. The world doesn't need another Andru Edwards or Casey Neistat. The world needs you to be fully *you*, so combine your experiences and personality quirks into something creative on YouTube.

YouTuber Sara Dietschy first rose to popularity by creating a parody of how-to vlogs like Casey Neistat. That video received two million views, and Casey liked it so much he mentioned it in one of his vlogs, linking to her channel and giving a boost to her growth.

Vlogger Amy Landino reviewed a book by Gary Vaynerchuk by creating a song and music video, earning Gary's attention. Both Sara and Amy thought differently. As a result, it helped them gain exposure, show appreciation to mentors and influencers in their lives, and build their influence on YouTube.

Just because you're committed to your channel's niche content doesn't mean you can't change the delivery. Even if you've been at it for a while, you can implement some changes to make your content more unique and help the channel grow.

Years ago, JP Sears started a self-help "talking head" channel, and he worked at it for almost two years. He only received a couple thousand video views per upload, so he sought our advice for what to do to accelerate his channel. Instead of telling him to stray from his current path, we advised him to keep it up, because that niche was an underserved part of YouTube.

JP is actually a very funny person, but he didn't think that aspect of his personality fit into his channel. However, he decided to embrace his own uniqueness. Shortly thereafter, Ultra Spiritual JP was born. The character covered the same types of content he'd already created, but he did it in a comedic way. The difference in audience reception was night and day. Viewers loved the new character. The change in delivery allowed him to expand his audience, and his channel grew from a few thousand views per upload to hundreds of millions of views across both YouTube and Facebook.

He didn't change his vision, he just pivoted his content, delivering the value he wanted but with a different presentation, and it made all the difference.

UP-LEVEL YOUR UNIQUENESS

In our interview with Charlie from *Charisma on Command*, he mentioned that he experienced a boost when he experimented with varying his content formats. Many YouTubers get into a rut, creating only one form of content over and over. They forget that every time they approach YouTube, they're approaching a blank canvas. The only limitation for what they create upon that canvas is their own creativity.

There are so many possibilities when it comes to creating content. Mix it up. One video could be animated with voiceover narration like a "draw my life" video. Another video could include mixed media, such as photos, videos, and music combined in unique ways. Maybe a few of your videos could be livestreams. As long as you're delivering the message you want to deliver, play with different formats.

With *Video Influencers*, we tried to think differently about helping people with online video tips by creating a weekly interview show. While we have many peers who share similar information and educational videos like *Video Influencers*, no one in our industry had created a weekly interview show up to that point.

The format wasn't unique in other industries. Many podcasts and YouTube channels use the weekly interview format to deliver regular content. But nobody had done it in our niche. That's the key.

How could you think differently about your content format to bring fresh creativity to your niche? How might you borrow innovation and creative ideas from other industries or niches?

One of the best ways to think differently and discover your unique positioning on YouTube is to scratch your own itch. What are the things you search for, and what kind of content do you wish was on YouTube? If it's something you're looking for but can't find, or if it's in a style that you would love but can't find, chances are other people would enjoy it as well. That could be a great guiding marker for you to carve out a unique space on YouTube.

As bestselling author and entrepreneur Sally Hogshead says, "Different is better than better." Being unique is so important, we hope these tips will help you shape your own voice and branding to stand out and grow faster.

QUESTIONS TO HELP YOU FIND YOUR UNIQUENESS

Consider these questions as a starting point to help you set yourself apart on YouTube:

- What is oversaturated in your niche? What small tweaks or changes could bring something fresh to a topic that's already established?
- What past experience could you combine with your current passion to create a unique channel?

- What are your biggest strengths, and are you currently incorporating them into your YouTube content?
- What do friends and family love about your personality? Are you fully letting your unique personality shine through on YouTube?
- What do you wish was on YouTube? Is there some topic or niche that you personally would love to watch that you haven't been able to find?

Over 2.3 billion people watch YouTube every month, and we believe billions more will come to the platform over the next decade. That means double the views and double the channel opportunities. "There's too much competition" and "It's too late" are excuses we've seen proven wrong time and time again since we started on the platform.

As *New York Times* bestselling author and marketing expert Seth Godin said, "You can either fit in or stand out, not both." To stand out, you must embrace your uniqueness, think differently, and pave your own path.

CHAPTER 15

. . .

NEW YOUTUBE FEATURES

"Expect change. Analyze the landscape. Take the opportunities. Stop being the chess piece; become the player. It's your move."

—TONY ROBBINS

There's nothing quite as fun as movie night. You sit down with family or friends, your favorite snack and beverage in hand, and immerse yourself in a drama, comedy, romance, or action movie. When we were growing up, we would drive to Blockbuster, the most popular video rental store, where we would explore the aisles, looking for some exciting new movie on VHS or DVD to watch. In those days, when you rented a movie, you got to keep it for two nights, but that meant if you failed to return the tape or disc back to the store in time, you accrued a late charge.

Depending on your age, you might remember the saying, "Be Kind, Rewind." Don't forget to rewind that VHS tape before you return it to the store! It takes a few minutes, but it's the nice thing to do for the next renter. This Blockbuster routine was an intrinsic part of movie night in the '80s and '90s, but streaming services (and the resulting demise of Blockbuster) have made that routine little more than a quaint memory for people of a certain age.

Yes, movie night has changed quite a bit over the years. Then again, visual media has only been around for about 120 years. The first silent short film premiered in Paris on December 28, 1895. By the 1930s, films had transitioned to color with synchronized sounds. In the 1950s, television became mainstream, and people could watch movies and shows from the comfort of their own homes. By the 1980s, home video was mainstream, and since then, we've seen the rise of DVDs, Blu-ray, and finally, streaming services.

As soon as human beings discovered the magic of visual media, the demand for new content took off, growing at a truly astonishing rate. In a sense, people still want exactly the same thing that they wanted back in 1895. They want to be entertained, to learn something, to laugh, cry, and relate to the human struggle through a powerful story. The basic human desire has never changed, but the way visual content is created and delivered has changed tremendously. And that, in turn, has changed the way people consume content. Today, the demand isn't just for two-hour movies or thirty-minute TV shows, because we now have thirty-second TikToks and YouTube Shorts.

You no longer have to get in your car and drive to the local video rental store. You no longer have to worry about returning that movie in time to avoid late fees because you can access content on-demand through Amazon, YouTube, Netflix, Hulu, and other services. Heck, YouTube is over sixteen years old now, and while it is considered a new media platform, it continues to grow and evolve at a rapid rate.

Because of these constant changes, if you're not careful, you can miss out on the new and evolving opportunities on the platform. That's exactly what happened to Blockbuster, after all.

THE TRAGEDY OF FAILING TO CHANGE

At its peak in the '90s, Blockbuster owned over nine thousand video rental stores in the United States, employed eighty-four thousand people worldwide, and had sixty-five million registered customers. In one year alone, they were valued at $3 billion, and the company earned $800 million in late fees alone.[39]

---

39 Andy Ash, "The Rise and Fall of Blockbuster and How It's Surviving with Just One Store Left," *Business Insider*, August 12, 2020, https://www.businessinsider.com/the-rise-and-fall-of-blockbuster-video-streaming-2020-1.

In September of 2000, Blockbuster was given the opportunity to purchase a strange new startup called Netflix for just $50 million. In his arrogance and lack of insight, Blockbuster's CEO, John Antioco, saw Netflix as little more than a big joke, so he passed on the opportunity.[40] A decade later, Blockbuster is long gone. The company filed for bankruptcy years ago with over $900 million in debt. At the same time, Netflix has flourished, and by 2020, the company was worth $194 billion.[41]

What's the moral of the story? Change before it's too late! When we created the Seven Cs framework for YouTube Success, it was designed to stand the test of time. The seven foundational principles will remain relevant for as long as YouTube exists. However, as every successful YouTube creator knows, you must be committed to the foundational principles of YouTube success while, at the same time, being willing to reinvent yourself, pivot your plan, and evolve along with the platform and audience viewing habits.

If you want to build a lasting legacy on YouTube, then you either adapt or die. Netflix adapted; Blockbuster died. You must be willing to change before it's too late.

40 Minda Zetlin, "Blockbuster Could Have Bought Netflix for $50 Million, but the CEO Thought It Was a Joke," *Inc.*, September 20, 2019, https://www.inc.com/minda-zetlin/netflix-blockbuster-meeting-marc-randolph-reed-hastings-john-antioco.html.

41 Ariel Shapiro, "Netflix Stock Hits Record High, Is Now Worth More Than Disney," *Forbes*, April 16, 2020, https://www.forbes.com/sites/arielshapiro/2020/04/16/netflix-stock-hits-record-high-is-now-worth-more-than-disney.

We want to help you do just that, so in this new chapter, we will explore some of the new features and significant changes that have come to YouTube since we published the first edition of our book. There are a few new ways to earn money and connect with an audience on the platform. In this chapter, we're going to tell you what they are and discuss how you can get the most out of them.

Then, at the end of the chapter, we have prepared some clarity questions to help you evaluate which of these changes and opportunities will best assimilate into your YouTube strategy. After all, just because someone created a shiny new tool doesn't mean it's the best use of your time.

On the other hand, you don't want to become so rigid in your ways that you refuse to embrace new and better ways of achieving success on YouTube. To that end, we're going to help you create a personal plan for dominating the platform in the next decade.

YOUTUBE SHORTS

The world is changing, and so is YouTube. Though the platform may well continue to dominate the video land-scape for years to come, many new competing video platforms have arisen and become popular. These new platforms focus largely on short-form content: quick, brief videos presented in a vertical format.

It's the younger generation who will define what the next decade holds for video content, and they've clearly voted. We've seen the rise of the TikTok craze, as young people embrace short-form content. Instagram saw this and took note, creating their own competing format called "Instagram Reels." And now, YouTube has followed suit, introducing something called YouTube Shorts. This new format allows creators to upload vertical videos of sixty seconds or less.

The numbers don't lie. According to a YouTube blog post in 2021, daily views of YouTube Shorts surpassed 6.5 billion globally within weeks of rolling out the new feature.[42] That's a huge audience hungry for more short video content. Remember, while you can watch Shorts on a desktop computer, they are primarily designed for mobile devices, and the YouTube app has been updated to integrate Shorts. Nevertheless, the young audience seems to love it.

How can you embrace all of these short-form video platforms? We've seen some successful creators repurposing their YouTube videos by taking out fifteen-second clips, reformatting them to vertical videos, and uploading them to YouTube Shorts, TikTok, and Instagram Reels. We don't normally recommend repurposing the same content to multiple platforms, but in this instance, it might be a

---

42   Todd Sherman, "Bringing YouTube Shorts to the US," YouTube Official Blog, March 18, 2021, https://blog.youtube/news-and-events/youtube-shorts-united-states/.

valuable way of reaching the primarily young audience that has fallen in love with this new format.

YouTube Shorts is not simply a gimmick. Creators are already experiencing massive success with it. Jake Fellman is a content creator who dabbled on YouTube over the years without gaining much traction, but he finally decided to start playing around with YouTube Shorts. At the time, it was still in beta, but he began uploading simple fifteen-second 3D graphics clips that he'd made.

His initial views, while not massive, were more than he expected, so he began uploading daily clips to the Shorts Player. Within a few weeks, he started gaining momentum—from thousands of views to tens of thousands and eventually millions. Within six months, Jake Fellman had accrued four billion video views and gained four million subscribers on YouTube using Shorts. While his success story isn't typical, many other creators are experiencing impressive growth through Shorts.

The good news is, it's incredibly easy for YouTube creators to begin uploading content to YouTube Shorts. Think about how hard it is to become a YouTube creator. Even with smartphone cameras replacing expensive camera equipment, and despite the availability of free video editing software, it still takes a lot of time and research to create, edit, and optimize your content.

However, creating content for YouTube Shorts takes seconds. Press the plus sign on the app and select "Create a Short." Then you can shoot, arrange, edit, add music and sound effects, and upload the finished product to the Shorts Player within minutes. It's that easy! Whether or not that short gets views still depends on the content, of course, but at least someone without much experience or gear can create and upload content quickly.

It's a much lower barrier to entry than getting started on YouTube, so almost anyone can try it out. Even seasoned influencers are leveraging this new format to reach a new audience. Business marketing coach Chris Do already has an established YouTube channel and audience, but he started using Shorts to create short clips as snapshots or takeaways from his videos. After just a few months, some of his Shorts have accrued millions of views.

Chris's channel, *The Futur*, sits squarely in the education category, and most of the videos are long-form tutorials and conversations. However, experimenting on YouTube Shorts has produced the most viewed video on his channel, a YouTube Short that has gotten fifteen million views in just two months.[43]

Who is YouTube Shorts well-suited for? Anyone and

---

43   The Futur, "Why Charging By the Hour Doesn't Make Sense," YouTube video, 0:58, https://www.youtube.com/watch?v=TxeEzZvVGUc.

everyone, but maybe not right now. For a new creator with no video editing experience, or someone who lacks resources, YouTube Shorts is a great way to get started quickly. You can learn the video creation process, figure out how to apply the perfect video recipe, and start gaining an audience with your short-form clips.

It can also be useful for a seasoned creator who wants to reach a new audience or connect with a whole new part of YouTube. Many creators, like Chris Do, create YouTube Shorts from their longer-form content to connect with people who prefer short content—people who might otherwise never learn about him.

If you have the time to create more content, there's a lot of opportunity on YouTube Shorts to reach people, but remember, it's not a shortcut to success or a get-rich-quick scheme. YouTube Shorts takes commitment and hard work to create quality content that people want to see. Some of the most successful YouTube Shorts creators upload one to five Shorts a day, while those who already have an established audience might only upload one to five a week.

BEST PRACTICES FOR YOUTUBE SHORTS

Here are some best practices for getting the most out of YouTube Shorts.

- **The Perfect Video Recipe Condensed:** As with any other video, you need to hook the attention of viewers on YouTube Shorts in the first second or two. Get right to the point, keep their attention throughout, and make them want more.

- **Use the Tools:** The availability of music is one of the reasons this format has taken off, so consider using the trending songs that YouTube provides for Shorts. Also, the special effects and text tools will level-up your Shorts to make them more compelling and entertaining.

- **Consistency and Volume:** It's easy to create content on YouTube Shorts, but consistency and volume are the name of the game. A whole lot of creators are uploading a lot of content, so you need to make sure you're uploading, too. If you want to connect with an audience, your uploading needs to be consistent. Since this is still a new format, the algorithm is trying to figure out which videos to recommend, so the more Shorts you put out there, the more opportunities you have that one of them will break out. Think of it this way: the more times a batter is up to bat, the more likely it is that he will hit a home run.

- **Your Main Channel or a New Channel?** It's a good question. Should YouTube Shorts be part of your main channel, or should it be a second channel? It all depends on your goals. If you have the time to manage it, creating a second channel could be smart. Lisa

Nguyen is a foodie creator with an existing channel who started a second channel on YouTube Shorts. By uploading to the second channel consistently, with two to five clips a day, she quickly gained a million subscribers and half-a-billion views in six months. In turn, her main food channel also gained additional viewers and grew. This is a great approach for established creators, but if you're new and don't yet have a big audience, it's probably better to keep your Shorts on your main channel. However, if you're worried about Shorts disrupting your regular content schedule and the format your audience is used to, consider making it a second channel.

The fact is, YouTube Shorts is going to continue growing over the next decade. It's almost certainly the biggest new opportunity on the platform, so while it may not become the primary part of your YouTube strategy, it would be a mistake to ignore it.

YOUTUBE LIVE

One reason why YouTube has become such a significant platform around the world is that viewers feel close to the content creators they subscribe to. Indeed, YouTube allows you to get as close to creators as you possibly can without being physically present due to a format called "Live Streaming." While YouTube Live isn't new to the platform, it has become far more significant since the publication of our first edition of *YouTube Secrets*. Creators are now using it in ways that are transforming their businesses.

YouTube Live is a way to "live stream" yourself on the platform directly, whether you're using the app to go live right from your device or using streaming software like Streamlabs, StreamYard, or OBS. One benefit of live streaming is that you don't have to edit the video. Plus, it will become a regular video on your channel if you choose to leave it up.

Like radio and TV talk and news shows, many smart creators are building live streaming studios (called "battle stations" in industry jargon) to broadcast all kinds of niche content, including daily stock trading and market reports, church services and religious programs, sports commentary, politics, news, celebrity and influencer gossip, and even 24/7 live streaming of bird nests, farm animals, and public spaces.

Many professionals, business leaders, and entrepreneurs use YouTube Live to answer questions from subscribers that are posted in chat or to conduct interviews through StreamYard or Zoom. Gaming live streams have been growing in popularity as well. According to Ryan Wyatt, head of YouTube Gaming, users watched one hundred billion hours of gaming content on the platform in 2020—twice as many hours as they watched in 2018.[44]

One of the best examples of YouTube Live comes from Emily Baker, the attorney we mentioned earlier who posts commentaries on trending legal topics and lawsuits. Most of Emily's content takes the form of live broadcasts, some of which are one, two, or three hours long. Her confidence and competence on the subject give her the "chops" to speak clearly on legal topics in a way that both informs and entertains. Some of her live streams get ten thousand concurrent viewers at any given time, and those live streams often go on to get hundreds of thousands of views on her channel.

YouTube Live is ideal for anyone who can entertain, inform, educate, and keep an audience's attention in real time. Your subscribers will love the idea of connecting with you live, but they still expect to get some value out of the time they spend with you. If you can do that, then YouTube Live is for you! You might be the greatest content creator in the world, but if your live stream is boring, it won't do your channel any good.

---

44 Nick Statt, "YouTube Gaming Had Its Best Year Ever with More than 100 Billion Hours Watched," *The Verge*, December 8, 2020, https://www.theverge.com/2020/12/8/22163728/youtube-viewers-100-billion-hours-gaming-videos-2020.

- **Optimize for YouTube Search and Discovery:** Your live stream will still show up on YouTube's suggested video list, and in some cases, it will also show up in search results, so make sure your title and thumbnail are compelling and speak to a need or want that viewers have.

- **Plan Your Live Stream:** While you should avoid making your live stream feel scripted, it's still important to make some plans beforehand. Identify your takeaway, at the very least. You might even plan the full show itinerary. Remember, there still needs to be a "value proposition" that defines what viewers can expect to get out of the live stream. For example, when Sean goes live on his *Think Media* channel, he uses a title and topic that would be effective for any video. He also uses visuals, including text and overlays, to emphasize his points, because they help keep viewers' attention. By preparing his talking points in advance and defining the key takeaway of the live stream, he can create something that works well as a live stream but also works well as evergreen content on his channel months or years later.

- **Start Your Show:** Recently, Benji launched the #VIshow, which streams live on Saturday mornings. In the show, he interviews guests about their journeys and advice on YouTube. Sometimes, he shares tips of his own. Sean created the show *Coffee with Cannell*, where he answers questions and interviews guests using StreamYard, all while enjoying some delicious single-origin coffee.

- **Don't Let the Tech Hold You Back:** The most powerful thing about live streaming is that you can start with simple tools on a shoestring budget and upgrade as you grow. Sean uses a simple USB mic, Cam Link capture card, camera, and easy-to-use StreamYard software in his home office for his *Coffee with Cannell* show. Keeping the tech simple allows him to run the show by himself and focus on the content and guests. To learn exactly how he does this, check out TubeSecretsBook.com/SimpleLiveSetup. Of course, you can splurge and build an entire live streaming studio, like Benji did in a converted garage. Check it out at TubeSecretsBook.com/LiveStudioTour.

- **Engage:** Viewers love the idea of seeing you in real time, so make sure to acknowledge them. Shout out people who comment in chat and give praise to the regular viewers of your show.

- **Start Before You're Ready:** Putting yourself on the internet live can be intimidating, so if you're nervous, we fully sympathize. There's no way to cover up your mistakes. It's all raw, real, and uncut. Yes, that's scary, but we encourage you to stretch yourself beyond your comfort zone. Dare to experiment with YouTube Live. You might be surprised at how powerfully it contributes to audience engagement and community building.

When it comes to dominating the next decade on YouTube, live streaming is going to play a major role in helping many creators scale their impact and growth. Don't be afraid to test the waters and put yourself out there!

YOUTUBE STORIES

Instagram, Facebook, Twitter, and LinkedIn all have a "stories" feature that allows creators to upload temporary fifteen-second vertical clips and share them with followers. YouTube recently jumped on the "stories" bandwagon. With most platforms, stories disappear after twenty-four hours, but YouTube Stories are unique because they don't disappear for seven days.

The YouTube's Stories feature is available to all eligible channels with over ten thousand subscribers. Once you qualify, you can create a story simply by pressing the plus button on your mobile app and selecting "Add to Your Story." Once a story has been created, it can be viewed on the YouTube app by tapping your channel icon.

Stories appear on your viewers' YouTube home page in between recommended full-length videos and also at the top of your mobile app screen. The feature is intended to let creators share casual short clips and photos with current subscribers, but they can be discovered by new people who could become new subscribers.

So, at this point, you may be wondering, "What's the difference between YouTube Shorts and YouTube Stories?" Let's clarify.

YouTube Shorts are quick, casual vertical videos that stay on your channel forever (unless you delete them). They have the potential to gain massive views and reach new people if you strategize and post them intentionally. YouTube Stories, on the other hand, disappear after seven days, so they are better suited for connecting with current subscribers.

TIPS FOR YOUTUBE STORIES

- **Upload One Story a Week:** It only takes fifteen seconds to record a quick update for your community, and perhaps another minute to add a little text and stickers. By uploading at least one story per week, you will have the best chance of getting to the front of the line in recommendations. Most creators overlook this feature, so keeping it top-of-mind can give you an advantage.

- **Use Video Stickers:** Video stickers allow you to share links to your own or other people's videos on YouTube. However, you are limited to sharing one of your own videos every seven days. All you have to do is record a fifteen-second vertical video on the YouTube app, add a video sticker, and select the video you want to share. Tell your community why you're sharing that particular video and encourage them to tap the sticker and view the video. It's another great way to send traffic to a new upload that your subscribers may have missed, but it's also effective at pointing people to older videos in your library.

- **Use the Channel Feature @Mention:** You can recommend other channels on YouTube by entering the @ symbol followed immediately by the channel name. Why is this useful? Because it allows you to shout out another channel that would add value to your community, or you can cross-promote a second channel of your own. Sean's main channel, *Think Media,* has grown to over 1.8 million subscribers, but he recently created a second channel, *Think Media Podcast*, where he shares deeper conversations about building a profitable business around your YouTube influence. Besides using Stories once a week to recommend a video on his main channel, he also recommends videos from the new channel, along with the channel itself, using the @mention feature. This has helped *Think Media Podcast* acquire forty thousand subscribers in a short time.

YOUTUBE COMMUNITY TAB

One of the coolest new ways to reach your audience is through the Community tab, which is a bit like a social media wall for posting updates with text, photos, and links to your videos. To unlock this feature, you need at least five hundred subscribers. YouTube will send a notification once you unlock it, though it may take up to a week to gain access.

Of course, you don't *have* to use the Community tab. Many creators achieve incredible success on YouTube without ever using Stories, Shorts, *or* the Community tab. However, these new features offer more opportunities for speeding up growth and creating deeper connections with your audience, especially if you use them strategically.

YOUTUBE COMMUNITY TAB TIPS

- **Polls:** In our opinion, polls are one of the best ways of using the Community tab. People love participating in polls, so they will often reach the largest percentage of your subscribers. Create multiple choice questions to get audience feedback on what video they want to see next, or use yes-or-no questions to get clarity on what they think about certain topics. This will keep your channel top of mind, while giving you valuable insights about the content you should create.
- **Personal Updates and Pictures:** Viewers connect deepest with creators who share their values and beliefs. While you can be as public or private about your personal life as you want to be, it can be powerful

to post life updates with family photos to your Community tab. If you're taking a break from uploading to rest or go on a vacation, let your viewers know and share a relevant photo. You can also give behind-the-scenes sneak peeks on an upcoming project. All of these are good ways to deepen your bond with your subscribers.

- **Promote Your Videos:** As with Stories, you can use the Community tab to send traffic to new uploads, older videos in your library, or other people's content that your audience might enjoy. YouTube makes it easy to share videos on a community post. Just click "Video" and add a link that includes the title and thumbnail. However, to get the most reach and engagement, while also sending traffic to your own videos, we recommend uploading an attention-grabbing square image and putting the link to your YouTube video in a caption, along with a short description. Sean posts daily on the *Think Media* Community tab, testing which types of posts are most effective. For some excellent examples of polls, personal posts, and video promotions, check out the Community tab on Sean's *Think Media* channel. Remember, as with all of these new features, the name of the game here is "capturing people's attention," and the Community tab gives you more ways to do just that.

NEW WAYS TO MAKE MONEY ON YOUTUBE

One distinction between YouTube and other creator platforms is YouTube's long-standing and reliable monetization tool AdSense. However, the platform has added additional tools for monetizing your content in recent years. Let's look at a few examples.

SUPER CHAT

Super Chat is a way for viewers to pay a creator through the chat window in a live stream or video premiere. It also highlights the viewer's comment and pins it to the top of the chat window. To unlock the Super Chat feature, your channel must be monetized and have at least one thousand subscribers. It's a little like the street musicians that you see busking in big cities. While they play in public, passersby can stop, enjoy the music, and leave a tip in their open guitar case. With Super Chat, viewers can leave a tip of one dollar up to five hundred dollars. Sounds pretty good, doesn't it?[45]

When you create great content that serves your audience and builds a dedicated community, your fans will want to support you, and Super Chat is a way for them to do just that. Don't forget to remind them about the Super Chat

---

45 Geoff Weiss, "YouTube Rolls Out 'Super Chat' Feature to 19 Additional Countries," Tube Filter, August 13, 2019, https://www.tubefilter.com/2019/08/13/youtube-expands-super-chat-19-countries/.

feature while you're live streaming. Let them know it's a good way to show their appreciation. We've seen creators, like fellow YouTube expert Nick Nimmin, make hundreds of dollars during a multi-hour live stream.

SUPER STICKERS

Similar to Super Chat, viewers can buy Super Stickers during a live stream or video premiere. Super Stickers are animated images that express greetings, congratulations, support, or other emotions in response to what's happening on screen. They appear right in the chat stream and remain pinned at the top for a period of time.

CHANNEL MEMBERSHIPS

Viewers can join your channel through a monthly paid membership to get members-only perks such as badges, emojis, and exclusive content. It's up to you to decide how much your channel will charge for these memberships, as well as how many membership tiers you're going to have. While prices vary by country, in the US prices range from $0.99 to $99.99 a month. At the time of this second edition, YouTube requires you to be in the Partner Program and have at least thirty thousand subscribers to qualify for channel memberships.

Emily Baker offers three membership tiers for her channel:

Supporter (five dollars per month), Enthusiast (ten dollars per month), and Advocate (twenty-five dollars per month). Supporters get access to a special chat feature. Enthusiasts get chat plus special live streams. Finally, Advocates get chat, live streams, and private Zoom calls with Emily. Her members also get loyalty badges and custom emojis to use during her public live streams, signifying that they are part of her inner circle of "Law Nerds."

Our friend David Foster has a channel called *Morning Invest*, on which he shares progressive news and finance information with his co-host Clayton Morris. Their daily live show offers memberships to loyal viewers that give access to discounted merchandise and exclusive live streams. Membership costs run the gamut from $1.99 to $50.00. Most viewers opt for the lowest level, but with five thousand members, and twenty more joining every day, memberships are bringing in a five-figure income on top of their other sources of revenue.

MERCHANDISE STORE AND MERCH SHELF

YouTube partners with companies like Teespring so you can create merchandise and sell it on your channel. You keep a percentage of the profits, and the merchandise shows up in a viewing window right below your videos.

To gain access to this feature, you must be in the Partner Program and have at least ten thousand subscribers. You also need a clean slate when it comes to community guidelines, so avoid getting any strikes on your channel.

YouTube has been rapidly adding new merchandise platforms, such as Spreadshop, Spring (Spri.ng), and Suzuri. As of this writing, there are over twenty-five retailers that integrate with YouTube's merch shelf.[46] Creating your own merch allows you to express your creativity, build community, and generate additional revenue for your online business. Just be sure to let viewers know when merch is available. Wearing your hats, t-shirts, hoodies, and other gear within your content is also a great way to promote and remind viewers about your merch.

WHAT IS YOUTUBE'S CUT?

Susan Wojcicki, CEO of YouTube, wrote a letter in January of 2021 titled "Our 2021 Priorities," in which she revealed that "Creators and artists are finding other new ways to connect with their audiences and diversify their revenue. Last year, the number of channels making the majority of their revenue from Super Chat, Super Stickers, or channel memberships on YouTube tripled."[47]

---

46   "Get Started with Merch on YouTube," YouTube Help, https://support.google.com/youtube/answer/9454088.

47   Susan Wojcicki, "Letter from Susan: Our 2021 Priorities," YouTube Official Blog, January 26, 2021, https://blog.youtube/inside-youtube/letter-from-susan-our-2021-priorities/.

While these new YouTube monetization features are amazing, they come at a cost. For example, channel memberships are free for creators to use, but YouTube takes 30 percent of the profits. So, if your membership costs ten dollars a month and you have a hundred members, then you're generating $1,000 in profit per month. However, YouTube will keep $300, and you'll get $700. This 70/30 split is true for Super Chat and Super Stickers as well, and it will most likely apply to any new features YouTube adds in the future.

We recommend counting the cost of using these features and weighing them against alternatives. For example, Patreon is a popular third-party platform for creators to build a base of monthly income by offering supporter perks and exclusive content. Unlike YouTube, Patreon only takes a 10 percent cut of the revenue, which is further divided into a 5 percent platform fee and a 5 percent payment processing fee.[48]

If you grew your monthly membership revenue to $100,000 using YouTube memberships, the company could take $30,000 of that revenue, but Patreon would only take $10,000. That's a lot more money in your pocket. However, Patreon isn't native to the YouTube platform.

48   Eric Peckham, "The Business of Patreon," *Tech Crunch*, February 12, 2019, https://techcrunch.com/2019/02/12/patreon-business.

While YouTube does allow you to promote third-party websites like Patreon, or even your own website, sending traffic away from YouTube may not make the algorithm happy. Keep that in mind. Also, it might be harder to move your superfans away from YouTube if you don't keep every feature under one roof.

We're not saying these third-party tools are better or worse. We're just encouraging you to research the pros and cons of any tool you decide to use, including the revenue split. Besides Patreon, there are other tools like SubscribeStar, Ko-Fi, and Buy Me a Coffee, and new ones are created on a regular basis. The creator economy is growing fast, and there are more ways to monetize your content than ever before, both from YouTube and from third-party developers.

YOUTUBE APP

If you haven't updated the YouTube App in a while, you should probably get current. Why? First, so you can experience YouTube videos, Shorts, Stories, and the Community tab from a mobile viewer's perspective to gain insights for creating your own content using these features. Second, by getting current with the YouTube app, you will gain access to all of these new features, as well as additional tweaks and content creation tools.

YOUTUBE STUDIO APP

The official YouTube Studio app (which is distinct from the regular YouTube app) makes it easier and faster to manage your channel. We consider it essential for creators and channel owners. Check out your latest stats, respond to comments, upload custom video thumbnails, schedule videos, get notifications, and more.

Unlike competing creator apps such as Instagram and TikTok, YouTube provides comprehensive analytics, giving you the best viewer insights and video data to help you optimize your content. Remember the analytics we discussed in the "perfect video recipe," such as clickthrough rate (CTR) and average viewer duration (AVD)? They're all available on this app. Furthermore, YouTube constantly releases updates to the app, giving more insights into your channel performance so you can make data-driven decisions about your next upload.

YOUTUBE KIDS APP

This app is made specifically for kids under thirteen years of age, providing a safe option for them to view relevant content. The channels and videos accessible on this app have been deemed appropriate for viewers in this age range.

The Kids app isn't a content creation tool, but it's a good

way to study how kid-friendly content is distributed and recommended. More than that, it has become massively popular. According to a report from the analytics company Apptopia, YouTube Kids beat out thirty-four other services, including Netflix, Twitch, Disney+, Hulu, Amazon's Prime Video, and its own parent app in viewership.[49] Let that sink in. Think about all of the people who use Netflix around the world. Well, vastly more people are using the YouTube Kids app. It's a huge opportunity!

This is a recent development. Kids have always liked YouTube, but the Kids app was number one in "time spent on app" in 2020, so clearly its popularity is growing even faster. Remember, the young people using the YouTube Kids app today will be tomorrow's consumers (and creators) on the regular YouTube platform.

EVALUATING OPPORTUNITIES AND CREATING YOUR SIMPLE GAME PLAN

Your biggest enemy as a YouTube creator is lack of focus. We see new creators falling into this trap all the time. Even established creators can lose their edge by spreading themselves too thin. The new opportunities mentioned

---

49 James Hale, "YouTube Kids App Sees More Usage Than All Major Video Platforms'—Including YouTube," Tube Filter, April 2, 2020, https://www.tubefilter.com/2020/04/02/youtube-kids-2020-downloads-watch-time-apptopia-braze/.

in this chapter are real, but they might not be right for your channel.

If you try to post two videos a week to YouTube, as well as two Shorts, a weekly live stream, a daily audience survey on the Community tab, regular YouTube Stories, and also regular posts on Instagram, TikTok, Facebook, and Twitter, you're on a fast track to exhaustion and burnout. Plus, the quality of your content will suffer.

To build a real business around your YouTube channel, there's a lot of behind-the-scenes work that needs to be done when you're not creating content. If you're burned out, much of that behind-the-scenes work won't get done.

Which new opportunities should you take advantage of, and which ones aren't for you? To help you decide which ones to embrace now, and which ones to hold off on, we've provided the following clarity questions.

1. How much time do you have to devote to YouTube and your online business each week?
2. What could you stop doing that isn't getting results so you could invest that time into experimenting with new opportunities?
3. Who is your ideal viewer, and what is the best content format for reaching them?

4. Who could you ask for help and delegate some tasks and responsibilities to in order to free up more time?
5. Is it time to hire someone part-time or full-time to take some of the administrative work, video editing, or YouTube channel management off your plate?
6. When can you block some time on your calendar to test and experiment with YouTube Shorts and YouTube Live?
7. Are there any channels in your niche or category getting remarkable results with one of these new features?
8. Which videos are getting the most views and generating the most money on your channel right now, and should you double down on what's working before starting something new?

Answering these questions might not be easy. As content creators, we're constantly managing the tension between competing things. For example, there's always tension between the hours we have available in a week and the additional opportunities on the horizon. There's tension between maintaining a healthy pace over the long haul and sacrificing sleep to jump on a new trend. There's tension between sticking to the tried-and-true format and stretching into new content formats. There's also tension between focusing on making your YouTube business profitable and taking a break to focus on family and personal issues.

Spend time reflecting on these clarifying questions, then

create a simple plan of action for your next season on YouTube. As Richard Branson said, "Business opportunities are like buses; there's always another one coming." Don't give in to FOMO: fear of missing out. It might be strategic to jump on the latest YouTube trend, or it might be a distraction.

A final framework we like to use when facing new opportunities comes from our friend Gary Vaynerchuk. He recommends figuring out how much time you have each week to work on your business or side hustle, then using 80 percent of that time to focus on tasks and activities that are generating results today, and the other 20 percent on research and development into new opportunities. That way, you will continue to grow your online business while preparing for tomorrow.

In the fast-changing world of YouTube and social media, there are no guarantees. You must be willing to take some risks on new features and new platforms because they might pay off and save you from Blockbuster's fate. Then again, the risk might lead to a dead end, but at least you will have learned a lot in the process. Plus, you only spent 20 percent of your time experimenting, which you can now direct to the next experiment.

It's truly a decade of new opportunities on YouTube, so decide which ones might be relevant for you, your channel, and your audience and start experimenting. Don't miss out on what the next few years have in store for content creators!

CONCLUSION

Thomas Edison, revered by many as America's greatest inventor, developed many devices that greatly influenced life around the world, including the phonograph, the motion picture camera, and a long-lasting practical electric light bulb. He's also famous for allegedly saying, "Opportunity is missed by most people because it's dressed in overalls and it looks like work."

In this book, we hope you've seen that we live in one of the greatest times in human history. The opportunity provided by online video to reach and connect with people around the world on free platforms with low-cost tools is something our grandparents could never have dreamed of. However, in times of massive opportunity, it's important to take massive action.

Before we part ways—and you get to work on your channel—we want to share a few final tips and strategies so you can fully seize the opportunity that is before you.

THE BIGGEST MISCONCEPTION ABOUT YOUTUBE SUCCESS

Being a YouTube influencer might look like it's all fun and play. However, we can tell you from experience, every YouTube creator, influencer, and success story has one common attribute: an amazing work ethic. They hustle, hustle, hustle. The number one piece of advice we can provide is that everything comes down to how hard you're willing to work to be successful on this platform.

People underestimate the amount of work it takes. The allure of YouTube success is misleading. If you reach success, you can earn money, get free products, travel the world, and live an exciting, exhilarating life. However, that's just what it looks like from the outside.

After interviewing hundreds of today's top video influencers, we see a recurring theme. All of them put an insane amount of work into their channels. When we talk about hustle, we mean consistency—consistently creating and optimizing your content, consistently engaging with people, and constantly learning and improving.

Benji's vlog channel has over 1.8 million subscribers. Many

people watch, and that has opened numerous doors of opportunity for us. He's incredibly grateful for everything that has happened, but after fun days with the kids or traveling to cool places, every night the video editing must happen. Business is taken care of, and it all starts over every day.

When subscribers stumble upon our channel, they don't realize we've been on YouTube for ten years. In that time, we've uploaded thousands of videos. In the last six years, we've vlogged almost every single day of the week. Across both of our channels we have uploaded thousands and thousands of videos. Through determination, commitment, and the right strategy, you too can experience huge success leveraging the power of YouTube. In this book, we've given you the steps.

In the first part of this book, we talked about the Seven Cs, which you must do continually as you go through the stages of growing your influence on YouTube—always tapping into a new level of *courage*, always *clarifying* and refining your message and brand, always improving your *channel*, always improving your *content*, always engaging with your *community*, always finding new ways of generating *cash*, and always staying *consistent*, realizing you must hustle your way to success. In the second part of this book, we shared some actionable tactics and creative ideas for growing your channel, including the perfect video recipe, leveraging trends, ranking your videos, and collaborating with other creative people.

By this point, you'll see that it takes a lot of work to build influence on YouTube, and that's why we encourage you to build it around something you love. "If you do what you love, you'll never work a day in your life." There will be times when you're tired, and it will feel like a grind, but devoting yourself to something you love will make it all feel worthwhile.

WHAT DO YOU LOVE?

Is this what you want to be doing? Is this what you're passionate about? For some, YouTube is a means to an end, a stepping-stone toward their true calling. However, it's so important to have a passion and love for the content you create and the people you help.

Despite how successful Benji's real estate channel was, he's no longer an agent in that industry. He left because he viewed it as merely a stepping-stone in the right direction. It helped fund his true passion, which is helping people...helping you. That's why we have become such great friends, because we share a similar passion and calling, and that's why we wrote this book.

Speaking of real estate, in 2020 an entrepreneur named

Levi Lascsak picked up a copy of the first edition of You-Tube Secrets. He read Benji's story and applied it to his new career as a real estate agent.

He started sharing information about the Dallas, Texas, housing market and doing neighborhood tour videos. His videos only got a few hundred to a few thousand views. Though this may seem modest in terms of impressions and has not made him "internet famous," he has generated hundreds of qualified leads and has been able to convert them into buyers and sellers for his real estate business. This has led to a million dollars in revenue for him and his business partner, Travis Plumb, in their first year in the industry.

No paid advertising. No cold calling prospects. No viral videos. Less than five thousand subscribers.

Over one million dollars in real estate commissions generated in less than a year.

Levi's story proves that it's not too late to start YouTube and you don't need a million subscribers to make it. You just need to start messy, work hard, and keep learning as you go. Do things always work out? Of course not. You may need to persevere longer or pivot your strategy. If you're struggling, ask yourself if you're truly doing what you love. At this point, you might feel overwhelmed. You've received a lot of information. Break it down and think about the next thing you need to do.

Maybe that's setting up your channel. Maybe that's posting your first video. Maybe it's scheduling a day to shoot your next batch of content. A commitment to these small actions compounds to big results. Little by little, a little becomes a lot.

THE TIMELINE FOR SUCCESS

The timeline is different for everyone, and it depends on your type of content, the makeup of your audience, your business model, the level of hustle you're willing to put in, and how quickly you can learn.

Be ambitious, but never get impatient. As the saying goes, *overnight success takes ten years*. We don't believe it has to take that long, but it might. For some, it could be quick. For others, it could take much longer. Always remember, you are on your own path. Never fall into the trap of comparing yourself to somebody else. Your race is your own.

Jerry from the tech channel *Barnacules Nerdgasm* didn't have breakout success until the seventh year of his career. John Kohler from *Growing Your Greens* had many slow years on YouTube of being consistent before his channel took off and experienced huge growth. It took Judy Travis two years of uploading videos and being denied three times from the YouTube Partners Program before she could monetize her channel. It then took another year before she could make it her full-time career.

Greatness takes time. While we don't believe anything great happens instantly, if you apply the tactics we've given you, you can shave off tons of time, avoid pitfalls, and get the most out of the energy you put in.

LEARNING DOESN'T STOP HERE

While we may be coming to the end of this book, it's only the beginning of our journey together. We want to invite you to be a part of the Video Influencers online community.

On our YouTube channel, we share even more strategies and tips. It's like a YouTube university that is completely free, and you can access it any time. Plus, we encourage you to look at our interviews with other YouTubers, business owners, entrepreneurs, and creatives from around the world to learn their best tips for growing your influence with video.

Additionally, in the appendix of this book, we've included answers to some of the top questions we receive. We also share quick tips and links for deeper training, all available online for free.

Always keep in mind your "why." Inspiration can be a spark of energy. Motivation can get you pumped up in the morning, but drive is what keeps you going. Drive is created by your why. Why are you creating videos? Why do you want to have a YouTube channel? Why do you want to achieve success on this platform?

Always make serving your audience your top priority and never forget why you started. It's ultimately not about you. It's about the people on the other side of the camera lens, on the other side of that internet connection, watching through their devices. You're ultimately creating content to make a difference in the lives of people, so if you get discouraged, always keep them in mind.

In this book, you've learned about the secret society and subculture that is YouTube and the massive opportunity that exists for you right here, right now. We've shared with you the tactics of the influencers who are getting results and creating lives, businesses, and brands on their own terms doing what they love, but remember: YouTube is a marathon, not a sprint. Stay focused on your vision. Put in the work. Keep building your influence, income, and impact, one video at a time.

APPENDIX

We've gotten a ton of questions, and we've done our best to include the best tips and strategies throughout this book. However, some things might not have been included, so we want to share the questions we get most often and provide succinct answers, along with additional resources you can find online.

HOW DO I GET MORE SUBSCRIBERS AND VIEWS?

This question is, by far, the one we hear most. Our biggest recommendation is to simply apply everything you've just learned in this book. Stick to the strategy and keep working these tactics. If you desire more training, check out this playlist on our YouTube channel: TubeSecretsBook.com/Grow.

HOW CAN I BUILD CONFIDENCE TO BE ON CAMERA?

The more knowledgeable and passionate you are about the subject, the more confident you'll feel talking about it on camera. Beyond that, practice is essential. The more times you get in front of the camera, record, edit, and upload your videos, the better you'll be. No athlete or musician performs perfectly on their first day, so don't be hard on yourself. Just remember that practice makes progress. Watch our best videos and tips for building your confidence to get on camera: TubeSecretsBook.com/Confidence.

HOW CAN I STAY MOTIVATED WHEN I'M NOT SEEING RESULTS YET?

Greatness takes time, and results don't happen overnight. Like working out at the gym, you don't get immediate, visible results. It takes time and consistency. For our best tips on staying motivated, along with some of the mindset hacks and daily practices that Benji and I use, check out this video playlist: TubeSecretsBook.com/Motivation.

HOW DO I DEAL WITH HATERS, TROLLS, AND NEGATIVE COMMENTS?

The number one thing you want to do when it comes to dealing with haters, trolls, and negative comments is to mentally prepare yourself for them. They are universal for all creators, from beginning YouTubers to seasoned creators, and even the superstars. Dealing with negative comments is a fact of life. For a few practical strategies on dealing with haters and negativity, check out these videos: TubeSecretsBook.com/Haters.

HOW DO I BECOME A DAILY VLOGGER?

Year after year, vlogging is growing in popularity, so we totally understand your aspiration to become a daily vlogger. However, it's not an easy path, and succeeding as a vlogger comes with some unique challenges. The path to becoming a vlogger doesn't necessarily start as a vlog channel. Most successful vloggers became famous for niche content, then started daily vlogging. If it's your ambition, check out these interviews with some of today's top vloggers: TubeSecretsBook.com/Vlog.

HOW DO I GET MY FIRST 100 SUBSCRIBERS?

Getting your first 100 subscribers can be as easy as asking your family and friends to support you. The average number of friends people have on Facebook is 250. Often, the people willing to support you are only a direct message, email, or phone call away. For some specific strategies for getting your first 100 subscribers on YouTube, check out this video: TubeSecretsBook.com/First100.

WHICH CAMERA SHOULD I BUY?

While we understand a quality camera is important, content value is always more important than production value. For most people, we recommend starting with your smartphone, which is adequate. The stories you tell and the value you add always supersede the technology you use. The best resource we have for you is Sean's channel, *Think Media*, which focuses on video production, live streaming, equipment, video editing, and tips for creating content. Check out this video: TubeSecretsBook.com/ThinkMedia.

HOW DO I COME UP WITH VIDEO IDEAS?

Just as writers experience writer's block, YouTubers experience "video idea block." It's something we all face. We keep a video idea list that we can reference whenever we have "video idea block." If you feel like you're stuck or in a rut when coming up with video ideas, we encourage you to check out this series of tips from *Video Influencers* to refill your video ideas tank: TubeSecretsBook.com/Ideas.

WHERE CAN I LEARN VIDEO EDITING?

Learning how to edit is as simple as getting started. Benji started with the most basic editing program that was preinstalled on his laptop. He had absolutely no knowledge, but he just started cutting scenes. Practice makes perfect.

Check out our recommended video editing apps and software for every device below:

- You can just get started with your smartphone. InShot is a great way to do that. TubeSecretsBook.com/InShot
- If you're using an iPad, we love LumaFusion, though it also works on iPhone. TubeSecretsBook.com/LumaFusion
- If you have an Apple computer and are just getting started, we recommend iMovie. TubeSecretsBook.com/iMovie
- If you have an Apple computer and want more functionality, we recommend Final Cut X. TubeSecretsBook.com/FinalCutX
- If you're using a PC, we recommend Adobe Premiere Pro. TubeSecretsBook.com/AdobePremiere

WHAT ARE YOUR TIPS FOR COLLABORATIONS?

Collaboration is one of the best ways to grow your channel, so we recommend rereading the chapter on collaboration in this book. You might wonder how we've been able to get so many interviews from top video influencers. For specific strategies on getting people to collaborate with you, check out this playlist: TubeSecretsBook.com/Collab.

ACKNOWLEDGMENTS

BENJI'S ACKNOWLEDGMENTS

Judy, I am forever grateful for your inspiration and love. You were, are, and continue to be the number one model of what is possible when it comes to being a YouTuber. Thank you for all you've done and have shown me is possible with this amazing platform called YouTube.

Sean, when I first met and hired you to film my proposal to Judy, I never imagined we would have written a bestselling book about YouTube a decade later. Your wisdom and integrity is only rivaled by your hard work ethic and tenacity to persevere. Thank you for all that you've done for my family and being one of my best friends on this journey!

SEAN'S ACKNOWLEDGMENTS

Steve Jobs said, "Great things in business are never done by one person. They're done by a team of people." I believe that is true in life as well, so as we publish the second edition of our book, it's especially important that I acknowledge the team that I value most in the world—starting with my amazing wife, Sonja Cannell. Thank you for your love, support and sacrifice on the journey of building our business together. As the co-founder and CFO of Think Media, your skills in money management and team leadership have been vital to the success we are experiencing today. Your faith, prayers, and encouragement over the years have been rocket fuel to help me crash through quitting points. Your wisdom and discernment helped me navigate complex business decisions and saved us millions of dollars. I would not be here without you. I am so grateful for you and love you so much.

Thank you Benji Travis for your friendship and partnership in Video Influencers and YouTube Secrets. Thank you Judy Travis for believing in me in the early days and always being generous with your influence by opening doors for others. You and Benji are world-class creators, parents, and humans. I'm honored to call you friends.

Thank you to Gabby Arciniega for serving the Video Influencers' community over the last six years by helping us pump out consistent content. Thank you Jordan Perez,

Chris Yost, Nouchaly Keo, Gabe Arciniega, and John Mediana for your help *with* Video Influencers over the years.

Big thanks to the entire Think Media team for your support, and thank you to Heather Torres for believing in our vision and being the glue that holds things together. Thank you Omar El-Takrori for your strong support and ride-or-die hustle for over a decade of video shoots, flights, weird hotels, and events. Thank you Kyle Anderson, Melissa Caputo, Isaiah Torres, Nolan Molt, and Jordan Perez for helping build Think Media in the early days.

I also want to thank my parents, Phil, Susan, and John; my stepbrother Allen Eskelin; and my extended family. I am who I am today because of your love, wisdom, prayers, generosity, and encouragement. Thank you from the bottom of my heart.

I also believe that mentorship is the key to extraordinary success. I want to thank Jeff Moors for getting me started in video production back in 2003 and helping me grow as a leader. Thank you Chalene and Bret Johnson for believing in me and challenging me to go to another level. Thank you David and Alice Goldstein, for your wisdom and encouragement. Alejandro Reyes for your friendship and all of the business brainstorm sessions. Benny Perez for the growth opportunities, leadership lessons, and helping me become a better communicator. To all the friends, teachers, pastors, bosses, and coworkers over the last fifteen-plus years, thank you for your influence on my life.

I also need to acknowledge some mentors who have coached me through books and content: Gary Vaynerchuk, Dave Martin, James Wedmore, Lewis Howes, Brendon Burchard, John Bevere, Kris Vallotton, and John Maxwell—just to name a few.

I want to thank the entire team at Scribe Media for making this book a reality, and I would be remiss not to acknowledge and thank the founders and team at YouTube. You have shaped history and given creators like us a platform to reach the world.

Thank you Rob Sandie and the entire vidIQ team for your friendship and for developing an incredible software, tools, and resources that have helped us grow our YouTube channels.

Finally, I want to thank Jesus Christ for the gift of life and salvation. I recognize that apart from Him, I can do nothing. Soli Deo gloria.

WANT TO CONNECT WITH SEAN AND BENJI?

It's been a crazy journey since we published the first edition of this book. *YouTube Secrets* has become the number one bestselling YouTube strategy book in the world. Thus far, it's been translated in Vietnamese, Chinese, Korean, Russian, Portuguese, and Ukrainian. Whether you've been a part of our journey from the beginning, discovered one of our videos over the last few years, or purchased this book randomly on Amazon, we thank you for your time and support.

Over the last few years, Benji and his wife Judy have been able to cross the one billion views threshold and continue to vlog daily after ten years on YouTube. They now have four beautiful girls and still live in the Seattle, Washington, area. During that time, Sean and his wife Sonja welcomed their first child into the world.

The best way to connect with Benji is at BenjiTravis.com or by following the @BenjiManTV handle on social media. He offers free thirty-minute consulting calls for full-time influencers who are looking to grow their brand and business in the creator economy. Also, he loves speaking at events and being a guest on digital conferences and trainings.

The best way to connect with Sean is at SeanCannell.com, where you will find many free resources for accelerating your success on YouTube and tips for building a profitable business around your online influence. You can also easily submit speaking requests and interview requests, and get information about his coaching and events. On social media, Sean is most active on Instagram and would love to connect with you. Tag @SeanCannell and use the hashtag #YouTubeSecrets, so he can re-share your post or story.

This next decade is going to be the best decade on YouTube. It's your time, and we're here to help. To your success!

ABOUT THE AUTHORS

 **BENJI TRAVIS** is a family man, You-Tuber, and business owner. He has surpassed over one billion video views through his channels and has experience building successful businesses on YouTube during his ten years on the platform. In addition to these entrepreneurial ventures, Benji and his wife (who is also a successful YouTuber) have raised over $2 million for charity by utilizing live broadcasting strategies. He has coached countless creators over the last decade, helping them grow their influencer businesses, and he can be reached at BenjiTravis.com. Reach out for speaking, coaching, and consulting requests.

 **SEAN CANNELL** is the CEO of *Think Media* and co-host of the *Think Media Podcast*. He is one of today's leading online video experts and the world's most watched YouTube strategist. Sean has been featured on Forbes.com, CNBC, Social Media Examiner, Entrepreneur.com, and Success. com. After growing a six-figure income as a "Tech YouTuber," he built a multimillion-dollar online video education company that he still runs today.

Sean is also an international speaker, coach, and prolific content creator. His mission is to help ten thousand purpose-driven people create a full-time living with YouTube.

He lives in Las Vegas with his wife Sonja, his son Sean Bradley, and his Chihuahua Sophie.

Get in touch at SeanCannell.com.